# Conscience Decides

# Conscience Decides

Letters and Prayers from Prison
written by

## Sir Thomas More

between April 1534 and July 1535

*Preface* by Rt Rev Trevor Huddleston, C.R.
*Introduction* by M. l'Abbé Germain Marc'hadour

Selected and arranged by
Dame Bede Foord of Stanbrook Abbey

GEOFFREY CHAPMAN
London                    1971

Geoffrey Chapman
18 High Street, Wimbledon, London SW 19

Geoffrey Chapman (Ireland)
5–7 Main Street, Blackrock, Co Dublin

First published 1971
© compilation 1971, Geoffrey Chapman Ltd

ISBN 0 225 65812 7

This book is set in 10 on 12 point and
11 on 12 point Intertype Plantin

Made and printed in England by
A. Wheaton & Co, Exeter, Devon

# CONTENTS

# ACKNOWLEDGEMENTS

This selection of *Letters and Prayers* has been taken from the first edition of *The Workes of Sir Thomas More, Knight*, printed in 1557 by St Thomas' nephew, William Rastell, son of his sister Elizabeth.

The excerpts from William Roper's *Life of Sir Thomas More, Knight*, have been taken from the edition published in 1910 by G. Bell and Sons, edited by George Sampson.

A good deal of the spelling and punctuation has been modernised, and, with a view to avoiding a congestion of footnotes, many of the words also. In a number of cases it seemed legitimate to exchange the obsolete word for the more modern equivalent, which St Thomas himself has used elsewhere. Occasionally the sequence of the words has been altered to accord with modern usage and make for easy and straightforward reading. Margaret always uses the plural 'you' when writing to her father, whereas St Thomas addresses her indiscriminately with 'you' or 'thou'; in most cases here, his 'thou', 'thee' etc. has been changed to 'you'.

I owe a very real debt of gratitude to the Right Reverend Bishop Trevor Huddleston, C.R., for kindly consenting to write the Preface, and to M. l'Abbé Germain Marc'hadour for his Introduction and his untiring help and advice. Indeed, my gratitude extends to all writers on St Thomas More.

# PREFACE

'When it becomes the "sacred duty" of a man to commit sin', wrote Reinhold Schneider, the German Catholic poet and historian, 'the Christian no longer knows how he should live. There remains nothing else for him to do but bear individual witness—*alone*. And where such witness is, there is the Kingdom of God.'

The quotation is used in fact, not of St Thomas More, but of a young Austrian peasant—Franz Jägerstätter—who, because of his Christian faith, refused to serve in Hitler's army and, after imprisonment during which his wife tried her utmost to persuade him to change his mind, and secured the support of both clergy and friends, was beheaded on 9 August 1943.

In the years that lie between those two acts of solitary witness, and even in the years that have followed the Second World War, how many others have accepted the call to obey conscience rather than expediency, God rather than Caesar?

Our age, with its different patterns of totalitarianism, whether they be based on ideology or race or military power, is one in which the conscience of the individual Christian is certain to be exposed to continuous threat. Because we happen also to live in a period when mass-communication makes it so much easier for those in the corridors of power to shape and mould public opinion, the individual, whoever he is, is even more vulnerable. It is impossible today to be unaffected by the 'climate of opinion', it is all-pervasive, penetrating every area of life, even the most strictly personal and private. And, because moral and ethical problems of great significance and complexity are being raised as a consequence of man's own inventiveness, of his discoveries in science and technology, the need for steadfastness in matters of conscience is greater than ever before. And the temptation to compromise is correspondingly greater also.

That is why St Thomas More, as he is revealed in these marvellous letters from prison, is so immensely significant for our generation. There are, it seems to me, certain specially relevant qualities which blaze out '. . . like shining from shook foil . . .' in what he writes here.

First and foremost is the evident fact that St Thomas' conscientious refusal to subscribe the oath, in contrast to the cheerful alacrity with which his friends and colleagues did so ('Master Doctor Latimer . . . walked with divers other doctors and chaplains of my Lord of Canterbury. And very merry I saw him, for he laughed . . .'), was a refusal determined long before he was summoned to Lambeth. It was the result of years, not of weeks or months, spent reflecting in the presence of God on the true meaning of authority. 'Either I must hold differently from the crowd', he had written in his *Utopia*, 'and then it would be safer for me to say nothing, or I must hold with them and thus help to further their madness.'

His was an 'informed conscience' because he understood the discipline of prayer. He knew whom to obey, when the time came, because of the years in which he had practised obedience secretly and therefore knew the difference between saying 'Lord, Lord . . .', and doing the Lord's will.

But the cost of More's steadfastness was a profound 'alone-ness'. To say that he was 'lonely' would be a misrepresentation of the facts, for never was there a saint more conscious of the God-given blessings of friendship and family-life. And, even in prison, he had contact with those (like his daughter Margaret) whom he loved most. Yet alone he certainly was at the level where it counted most: the knowledge that the great majority even of those closest to him believed his refusal to subscribe to be a quirk of conscience and a scruple.

Finally, and this is to me the most glorious thing of all, the person who demanded his submission, that evil man King Henry—perhaps the nearest that English history can come to the dictator-tyrants of our day—was, to the end, the object of More's personal loyalty and love. The command 'Love your enemies; do good to those that hate you' has, perhaps, never been more perfectly obeyed.

What then have these letters to tell us today?
I believe that the Church of God is being called

supremely to be a community which will bear witness to Truth when, on all sides, Truth is under massive attack. This witness will, in some situations, demand heroism and more: in all situations it will demand steadfastness. But the individual Christian will increasingly feel alone and isolated in his witness. He will often be tempted to react to the evil pressures around him by hatred, not for the evil but for the human instruments of that evil.

Thomas More, the saint who combined so easily and so gracefully greatness and goodness, humanity and holiness, is the man to turn to in our need. I am sure that these letters will help many ordinary Christians, and others, to do just this.

✠ Trevor Huddleston, C.R.
*Bishop of Stepney*

# INTRODUCTION

Speaking of the Fathers of the Church, whose biographies he was writing or editing, Newman said that their letters were: 'Just that kind of literature which, more than any other, represents the abundance of the heart; which, more than any other, approaches to conversation' (*Historical Sketches*, II, 222).

This is especially true of a man like St Thomas More, who, as Erasmus said, enjoyed nothing in life so much as conversing open-heartedly—'communing' is the Tudor verb—with those who shared his views and interests. No wonder, then, that his letters hold a privileged place in all good selections from his works, and in the best biographies of him. They were also Robert Bolt's prime source for the play, *A Man For All Seasons*.

More's prison letters have a specific flavour and an exceptional ripeness about them. They are indicative of his state of soul when it is forced to new heights. Not only do they approach to conversation, nearly all of them are actually the continuation of an oral dialogue: 'As I have often told thee, Meg . . .'; 'I have sundry times shewed you. . . .'

Though the writer is a conscious and consummate

13

artist, his prison letters are strikingly simple and unadorned. They are addressed to the maids and little ones, as well as to Margaret. 'All' is a word that recurs continually in them: the Christian gentleman, if we may quote Newman again, 'has his eyes on all his company'. His wife, Lady Alice, is given due priority—'recommend me to my shrewd wife above all . . .'—but no one is left out of the picture. The easiest and loveliest of epithets, 'good', occurs here more often than any other. If letters are the mirror of the soul, goodness is clearly reflected here.

Margaret Roper—'Megg', 'Marget', 'daughter Margaret', he even calls her 'daughter Roper'—is the prisoner's main interlocutor. She had been his closest confidante for years. At this time she was nearing thirty, the age her father was when he started his literary career. Some phrases in her letters are direct echoes of the letter she is answering. 'Mine own good father' responds to 'mine own good daughter'. 'No little' resembles 'not a little' and 'not a few' in the opening sentence of More's previous letter. He was fond of these negative patterns.

Imitation is the highest form of praise, especially when—as is probably the case here—it is unconscious. The style is the man. The deep similarity between the two writers reveals the likeness of their minds and souls. As Chambers pointed out, Margaret's letter to Alice, reporting her *tête-à-tête* with their father in his cell, is unmistakably More, and yet it may be that its every word was penned by Margaret. The inclusion of her letters in this selection is the first of several features which make the Stanbrook edition different from the *Selected Letters* edited by E. F. Rogers (*The Works of St Thomas More*, Yale University Press).

Another difference is the extent of modernisation. More's voice, heard at this distance in time, is not always clear. Ridding the text of its ambiguities or obscurities, in order to remove hurdles from the reader's path, is a tradition as old as English printing: the texts of Chaucer and Higden which the young More used in the fifteenth century had been up-dated by Caxton.

The prison prayers—another original feature of this collection—are in little need, if any, of modernisation. Theirs is a less periodic style. They have the neat contours of something well chiselled. The most famous of them—'Give me thy grace, good Lord . . .'—reads like a litany. Others of his prayers are patterned on the collects of the missal and breviary. Every single word in them is carefully weighed, they should not be passed over casually or taken for granted, otherwise their sterling quality will be missed by those who repeat them after him.

More's whole personality comes to life in these letters and prayers. He was never colossal or titanic; even in his halcyon days he was always our size of a man. Here, in this last year of his life, there was no blunting of the sharp edge of his acumen, no damping of his blithe spirit, no waning of his powers of expression; he was only more frail in body and more vulnerable in nerve. Socially he was approaching zero: the brilliant discoverer of Nowhere[1] had become almost Nobody. His judges were soon to refer to him as 'a certain Thomas, lately of Chelsea', as they labelled the Bishop of Rochester 'John Fisher, clerk'. To Audley he is 'a foolish scrupulous ass', to others a monster of pride, to the King a traitor, to most of his friends and to his family an unfathomable riddle. Roper did not understand him when he said: 'The field is won.' Even Margaret failed to grasp his motives. They were disconcerted, as the disciples had been by Christ's attitudes and sayings, before they had fully imbibed his spirit.

For all the pious care of his family, not all of More's prison letters have survived. His great-grandson, Thomas More the priest, tells us in his *Life of More*, edited posthumously by his brother Cresacre: 'My father left me one, which was to his wife.' This is not extant, and yet it was prized, since it was 'afterwards drawn over . . . with ink' to keep the coal from becoming illegible.

During his fifteen months in the Tower, More was aged 57 to 58. Physically his autumn was short, and he was to die a worn old man. But his spiritual autumn was an unbroken glory. All passion spent, all sting and sharpness gone, nothing remained but the full array of what St Paul lists as 'the fruit of the spirit': 'charity, joy, peace, patience. . . .' He seemed to have espoused the world because he had dodged none of its tasks. While he had reaped some of its rewards, he felt he had also picked up some of its dust and dirt, and was

[1] Nowhere—the meaning of the word Utopia.

thankful to heaven, and even to Henry, for wrenching him out of the world: how cheerfully he forfeits it, and all his dear ones, 'for the winning of Christ'!

With all the documents that tell us about him it is not hard to approve of St Thomas, or to admire him. May he, a gentle persuasive advocate, teach us how to play all our cards, and how to speak to God; shame us out of our mediocrity; help us towards the solution of problems not unlike those of his own day, and brace us for ordeals perhaps as frightening as those he faced and went through so bravely. 'The things, good Lord, that I pray for, give me thy grace to labour for.'

Abbé Germain Marc'hadour
*Professor of the Catholic University of*
*Angers, France*
*International Secretary of* Amici Thomae Mori
*Editor of* Moreana

# LETTERS FROM PRISON
April 1534–July 1535

# PREAMBLE

On 30 March 1534, Parliament passed an Act settling the succession to the throne on the children of Anne Boleyn, whom Henry VIII had married in secret the previous November. Commissioners were then appointed to administer the new oath of allegiance. On 3 April the news reached London that the Pope in Consistory, with twenty-two unanimous cardinals, had finally decided the King's Great Matter, giving their verdict that Katherine of Aragon was truly the King's lawful wife. The King's commissioners at once shaped the form of the oath to include a clause by which those taking it abjured all foreign potentates. This was intended to mean the Pope, so that those who signed it were rejecting the Pope's authority, though few would realise this at first.

A fortnight later, on Low Sunday, Sir Thomas More went to St Paul's with Will Roper, his son-in-law, to hear the sermon. On their way home afterwards they called at the Old Barge in Bucklersbury. This had been his own house before he moved to Chelsea, and was now the home of John Clement, once tutor to Sir Thomas' children, and Margaret, his wife, who had been brought up in the More house-

21

hold. It was in this house, full of memories, as he sat relaxed and happy, that the commissioners' messenger found him, and straightway delivered to him a summons to appear before them the very next day at Lambeth Palace, there to take the oath. Not a single other layman was so summoned; all the rest were clergy.

Early on Monday morning Sir Thomas went down to his parish church for confession, Mass and communion; the family well knew this custom of his whenever he had a weighty matter in hand. In fact, this appears to have been the last Mass and communion of his life; perhaps he was thinking of it when he wrote, later on, in his prison prayers about communion: 'Let us not lose the time therefore, suffer not this occasion to slip, for we can little tell whether we shall ever get it again, or never.' (See p. 105.)

The parish priest at Chelsea was John Larke, D.D., a familiar friend, who would also die a martyr.

But when the time came for him to leave home, Sir Thomas changed his customary routine with his family. As a rule he would let them all conduct him to his barge, kiss them there on the landing-stage and wave goodbye as he moved off down the river; he loved them dearly and it always cost him to leave them for however short a time. On this last morning, when he knew he would never see his happy home again, he stopped them at the garden gate and closed it before they could come through, shutting them all from him.

With a heavy heart he went on towards the river,

followed by Will Roper for companion, and no one on the landing-stage to wave goodbye. Sad and silent he sat in the boat, as they slid off downstream, but suddenly he leaned towards Will and whispered in his ear, 'Son Roper, I thank our Lord the field is won', meaning that he had conquered his natural grief and heartbreak at being parted from his family, and would not let it weigh him down any more.

At Lambeth, Cranmer the Archbishop, Audley the Lord Chancellor and Cromwell the King's Secretary, picked out Sir Thomas first to have the oath tendered to him. He read it carefully, and then declared he could not sign it, so he was sent away to think it over by himself. He stood at a window where he could watch all the others arriving, and then departing in cheerful mood after having signed. He must have known nearly all of them, many were his good friends, whom he was thus forced to watch as they followed the line of least resistance. The one person he never saw, and was never allowed to see, was the only other on this occasion who refused to sign—the Bishop of Rochester, John Fisher.

Since he would not change his mind he was ordered into the custody of the Abbot of Westminster, and presumably spent the next four days in the Abbey. During this tense period of waiting, while the King and Council decided what should be the next step towards breaking down his resistance, Sir Thomas wrote to his eldest daughter a long account of the whole proceeding at the Palace, from the first moment of his arrival, all through the long argument, till his last words to the Lord Chancellor and Master Secretary that he would not swear against his conscience, that he had never stopped any man from taking the oath, nor advised any to refuse it, nor ever put any scruple in any man's head, which seemed to him good reason why he in his turn should be left to follow his own conscience.

# LETTER I

## TO Margaret Roper

The first letter was probably written from Westminster Abbey, during the four days in which Sir Thomas was held in the custody of the Abbot, 'my Lord of Westminster'.

When I was before the Lords at Lambeth, I was the first that was called in, albeit that Master Doctor the Vicar of Croydon was come before me, and divers others. After the cause of my sending for declared unto me, (whereof I somewhat marveled in my mind, considering that they sent for no more temporal men but me) I desired the sight of the oath, which they showed me under the great seal. Then I desired the sight of the Act of Succession, which was delivered me in a printed roll.

After reading which, secretly by myself, and considering the oath with the act, I showed unto them that my purpose was not to put any fault either in the act or any man that made it, or in the oath or any man that swore it, nor to condemn the conscience of any other man. But as for myself, in good faith, my conscience so moved me in the matter that though I would not deny to swear to the succession, yet unto the oath that was there offered me I could not swear without the jeopardising of my soul to perpetual damnation. And that if they doubted whether I did refuse the oath only for the sake of my conscience, or for any other fantasy, I was ready therein to satisfy them by mine oath. Which if they trusted not, what should they be the better to give me any oath? And if they trusted me that I would therein swear true, then trusted I that of their goodness they would not move me to swear the oath that they offered me, perceiving that to swear it was against my conscience.

Unto this my Lord Chancellor said that they all were sorry to hear me say thus, and see me refuse the oath. And they all said that on their faith I was the very first that ever refused it; which would cause the King's Highness to conceive great suspicion of me and great indignation towards me. And therewith they showed me the roll, and let me see the names of the lords and the commons which had sworn, and subscribed their names already.

Which notwithstanding, when they saw that I refused to swear the same myself, not blaming any other man that had sworn, I was in conclusion commanded to go down into the garden, and thereupon I tarried in the old burned chamber that looks into the garden and would not go down because of the heat. In that time I saw Master Doctor Latimer come into the garden, and there he walked with divers other doctors and chaplains of my Lord of Canterbury, and very merry I saw him, for he laughed, and took one or two about the neck so handsomely, that if they had been women I would have considered he were waxing wanton.

After that came Master Doctor Wilson forth from the lords and with two gentlemen was brought by me, and gentlemanly sent straight unto the Tower.[1] What time my Lord of Rochester was called in before them, that I cannot tell. But at night I heard that he had been before them, but where he remained that night, and so forth till he was sent hither, I never heard.

I heard also that Master Vicar of Croydon, and all the rest of the priests of London that were sent for, were sworn, and that they had such favour at the council's hand that they were not lingered nor made to dance any long attendance to their travail and cost, as suitors were sometimes wont to be, but were sped apace to their great comfort so far forth that Master Vicar of Croydon, either for gladness or for dryness, or else that it might be seen *quod ille notus erat pontifici*[2] went away to

---

[1] Dr Nicholas Wilson, chaplain and confessor to the King, at first refused to sign, but later took the oath and was released from prison.

[2] 'That he was known to the high priest' (John 18:15).

my Lord's buttery bar and called for a drink *valde familiariter*.[1]

When they had played their pageant and were gone out of the place, then was I called in again. And then it was declared unto me what a number had sworn ever since I went aside, gladly, without any sticking. Wherein I laid no blame on any man, but for my own self answered as before. Now, as well before as then, they somewhat laid unto me for obstinacy, that whereas before, since I refused to swear, I would not declare any special part of that oath that discontented my conscience and open the cause wherefore. For thereunto I had said to them that I feared lest the King's Highness would, as they said, take displeasure enough towards me only for the refusal of the oath. And that if I should open and disclose the causes why, I should therewith but further exasperate his Highness, which I would in no wise do, but rather would I abide all the danger and harm that might come towards me than give his Highness any occasion of further displeasure than the offering of the oath unto me of pure necessity constrained me.

Howbeit when they divers times imputed this to me for stubbornness and obstinacy that I would neither swear the oath nor yet declare the causes why, I inclined thus far towards them that rather than be accounted for obstinate I would, upon the King's gracious leave, or rather his such com-

[1] With great good fellowship.

nandment had, as might be my sufficient warrant
that my declaration should not offend his Highness, nor put me in the danger of any of his
statutes, I would be content to declare the causes
in writing; and more than that, to give an oath in
the beginning that if I might find those causes
answered by any man in such wise as I might
think mine own conscience satisfied, I would after
that with all mine heart swear the principal oath,
too.

To this I was answered that though the King
would give me license under his letters patent, yet
would it not serve against the statute. Whereto I
said that yet if I had them, I would stand unto the
trust of his honour at my peril for the rest. But
yet I think that if I may not declare the causes
without peril, then to leave them undeclared is no
obstinacy.

My Lord of Canterbury taking hold upon what
I had said, that I condemned not the conscience
of those who swore, said unto me that it appeared
well that I did not take it for a very sure thing and
a certain that I might not lawfully swear it, but
rather as a thing uncertain and doubtful. But then
(said my Lord) you know for a certainty and a
thing without doubt that you be bound to obey
your sovereign lord your King. And therefore are
you bound to leave the doubt of your unsure conscience in refusing the oath, and take the sure way
in obeying your prince, and swear it. Now, even
though in mine own mind I thought myself not

included, yet this argument seemed to me suddenly so subtle and named with such authority coming from so notable a prelate's mouth, that I could answer nothing thereto, but only that I thought myself I might not well do so, because in my conscience this was one of the cases in which I was bound not to obey my prince, since whatsoever other folk thought in the matter (whose conscience and learning I would not condemn nor take upon me to judge), yet in my conscience the truth seemed on the other side. Wherein I had not informed my conscience either suddenly or slightly but by long leisure and diligent search for the matter. And truly if that reason holds, then have we a ready way to avoid all perplexities, for in whatsoever matters the doctors stand in great doubt, the King's commandment given upon whichever side he likes, resolves all the doubts.

Then said my Lord of Westminster to me that howsoever the matter seemed to mine own mind, I had cause to fear that mine own mind was erroneous when I see the great council of the realm determine the contrary of my mind, and that therefore I ought to change my conscience. To that I answered that if there were no more but myself upon my side and the whole Parliament upon the other, I would be sore afraid to lean mine own mind only against so many. But on the other side, if it so be that in some things for which I refuse the oath, I have (as I think I have) upon my part as great a council and a greater too, I am

ot then bound to change my conscience and con-
orm it to the council of one realm, against the
eneral council of Christendom. Upon this Master
Secretary (as he that tenderly favoureth me), said
and swore a great oath that he had rather that his
own only son (who is of a truth a goodly young
gentleman, and shall I trust come to much wor-
ship) had lost his head than that I should thus
have refused the oath. For surely the King's Highness would now conceive a great suspicion against
me, and think that the matter of the nun of Canterbury was all contrived by my drift.[1] To which
I said that the contrary was true and well known,
and whatsoever should mishap me it lay not in my
power to help it without peril of my soul.

Then did my Lord Chancellor repeat before me
my refusal unto Master Secretary, as to him that
was going unto the King's grace. And in the re-
hearsing his Lordship repeated again that I
denied not but was content to swear to the succession. Whereunto I said that as for that point I
would be content if I might see my oath in that
point so framed in such a matter as might stand
with my conscience.

Then said my Lord: Marry, Master Secretary
mark that too, that he will not swear that either

[1] Elizabeth Barton, supposed to have had trances, in one of
which she prophesied that the King would not be king in
seven months if he married another woman. More warned
her, and told her to keep to 'things as may be profitable
to the soul' and not to meddle with such matters.

except in a certain manner. Verily no, my Lord, said I, but that I will see it made in such wise first as I shall myself see that I shall neither be forsworn nor swear against my conscience. Surely as to swear to the succession I see no peril, but I thought and think it reason that to mine own oath I look well myself, and be of counsel also in that way. I never intended to swear for a piece and set my hand to the whole oath. Howbeit, so help me God, as touching the whole oath, I never withdrew any man from it, nor ever advised any to refuse it, nor ever put, nor will, any scruple into any man's head, but leave every man to his own conscience. And I think in good faith that so were it good reason that every man should leave me to mine.

## LETTER II

### TO Margaret Roper

Four days later, on Friday, 17 April, having still refused to sign, Sir Thomas was taken to the Tower by boat. Under the Traitor's Gate he went, and the Lieutenant of the Tower was there to receive him as he landed. The porter made his customary demand to have the prisoner's 'upper garment'—a form of entrance fee—and Sir Thomas light-heartedly handed him his hat as his 'uppermost garment', saying he was sorry it was no better. But the porter solemnly declared it was his gown he must give up.

Very soon Sir Thomas set himself to quieten his family in their anxiety about him, knowing the despondency they would be in on hearing the news of his imprisonment. This, his first letter from the Tower, is to his daughter Margaret, to let her know how he is and how much he is thinking of them all. It is written with a piece of charcoal, for lack of a pen. He was short of paper too, but seems to have found a second piece on which to add a long postscript.

Mine own good daughter,

Our Lord be thanked, I am in good health of body and in good quiet of mind; and of worldly things I no more desire than I have. I beseech him make you all merry in the hope of heaven. And such things as I somewhat longed to talk with you all concerning the world to come, our Lord put them into your minds, as I trust he doth, and better too, by his Holy Spirit, who bless you and preserve you all.

Written with a coal by your tender loving father, who in his poor prayers forgetteth none of you all, nor your babes, nor your nurses, nor your good husbands, nor your good husbands' shrewd[1] wives, nor your father's shrewd wife neither, nor our other friends. And thus fare you heartily well for lack of paper.

Thomas More, Knight

Our Lord keep me continually true, faithful and plain[2] to the contrary whereof I beseech him heartily never to suffer me to live. For, as for long life—as I have often told thee, Meg,—I neither look for nor long for, but am well content to go if God call me hence tomorrow. And I thank our Lord I know no person living that I would had one fillip[3] for my sake, of which mind I am more glad than of all the world beside. Recommend me to your shrewd Will and mine other sons, and to

---

[1] Able, clever.    [2] Steadfast.    [3] A flick of the finger.

John Harris[1] my friend, and yourself knoweth to whom else, and to my shrewd wife above all, and God preserve you all, and make and keep you his servants all.

[1] His secretary. He married Dorothy Colly, Margaret Roper's maid.

LETTER II, TO MARGARET ROPER

# LETTER III

## TO Margaret Roper

Unable to bear the separation from her father any
longer, Margaret wrote to him begging him to take
the oath, and then tempted him still further by
saying she had taken it herself. This she had done
'as far as it would stand with the law of God',
hoping that by this step Cromwell would be persuaded to lift the ban on her visiting the prisoner
in his cell. Much saddened by her persistence, her
father replied:

Our Lord bless you.

If I had not been, my dearly beloved daughter,
at a firm and fast point this good great while
before, your lamentable letter had not a little
abashed me, surely far above all other things, of
which I hear divers times not a few terrible towards me. But surely they all touched me never
so near, nor were so grievous unto me, as to see
you, my well-beloved child, in such vehement,
piteous manner, labour to persuade me unto that
thing wherein I have of pure necessity for respect

36

unto mine own soul so often given you so precise answer before.

Wherein as touching the points of your letter I can make none answer, for I doubt not but you well remember that the matters which move my conscience I have sundry times showed you that I will disclose them to no man. And therefore, daughter Margaret, I can in this thing no further, but like as you labour me again to follow your mind, to desire and pray you both again to leave off such labour, and with my former answers to hold yourself content.

A deadly grief unto me, and much more deadly than to hear of my own death (for the fear thereof, I thank our Lord, the fear of hell, the hope of heaven and the passion of Christ daily more and more alleviate) is that I perceive my good son your husband, and you my good daughter, and my good wife, and mine other good children and innocent friends, in great displeasure and danger of great harm thereby. The let[1] whereof, while it lieth not in my hand, I can no further but commit all unto God. *Nam in manu Dei*, saith the scripture, *cor regis est, et sicut divisiones aquarum quocunque voluerit, impellit illud*[2], whose high goodness I most humbly beseech to incline the noble heart of the King's Highness to the tender favour of you all, and to favour me no better than God and

[1] Hindrance, prevention.
[2] The king's heart is a stream of water in the hand of the Lord; he turns it wherever he will. (Proverbs 21:1.)

myself know that my faithful heart towards him and my daily prayer for him, do deserve. For surely if his Highness might inwardly see my true mind such as God knoweth it is, I would (I trust) soon allay his high displeasure. Which while in this world I can never in such wise show but that his Grace may be persuaded to believe the contrary of me, I can no further go, but put all in the hands of him, for fear of whose displeasure for the safeguard of my soul stirred by mine own conscience (without insectation[1] or reproach laying to any other man's) I suffer and endure this trouble. Out of which I beseech him to bring me, when his will shall be, into his endless bliss of heaven, and in the meanwhile, give me grace and you both in all our agonies and troubles, devoutly to resort prostrate unto the remembrance of that bitter agony which our Saviour suffered before his passion at the Mount. And if we diligently so do, I verily trust we shall find therein great comfort and consolation. And thus my dear daughter the blessed spirit of Christ for his tender mercy govern and guide you all, to his pleasure and your weal[2] and comforts both body and soul.

Your tender loving father,<br>Thomas More, Knight.

---

[1] Censorious criticism.     [2] Well-being.

# MARGARET ROPER'S LETTERS TO THOMAS MORE AND TO ALICE ALINGTON

This is Margaret's answer to her father's letter, in which she refrains from mentioning the sore point of the oath:

Mine own good Father,

It is to me no little comfort, since I cannot talk with you by such means as I would, at the least way to delight myself in this bitter time of your absence by such means as I may, by as often writing to you as shall be expedient, and by reading again and again your most fruitful and delectable letter, the faithful messenger of your very virtuous and ghostly[1] mind, rid of all corrupt love of worldly things, and fast knit only in the love of God and desire of heaven, as becometh a very true worshipper and a faithful servant of God, who I doubt not, good father, holdeth his holy hand over you and shall—as he hath—preserve you both body and soul now when you have rejected all earthly consolations and resigned yourself

---

[1] Spiritual.

willingly, gladly and fully for his love to his holy protection.

Father, what think you hath been our comfort since your departing from us? Surely the experience we have had of your life past, and godly conversation, and wholesome counsel, and virtuous example; and assuredly not only of the continuance of that same, but also a great increase, by the goodness of our Lord, to the great rest and gladness of your heart devoid of all earthly dregs, and garnished with the noble vesture of heavenly virtues, a pleasant palace for the Holy Spirit of God to rest in, who defend you from all trouble of mind and of body, and give me, your most loving obedient daughter and handmaid, and all us your children and friends to follow that which we praise in you, and to our only comfort remember, and communing together of you, that we may meet with you, mine own dear father, in the bliss of heaven, to which our most merciful Lord hath bought us with his precious blood.

> Your own most loving obedient daughter and bedeswoman[1] Margaret Roper, who desireth above all worldly things to be in John a Wood's[2] stead to do you some service. But we live in hope that we shall shortly receive you again, I pray God heartily we may, if it be his holy will.

[1] One who prays for another.
[2] Thomas More's personal servant who was allowed to attend on him in prison.

Eventually Margaret was successful in obtaining
the King's licence to visit her father. No doubt, the
fact that she had signed the oath herself was a con-
siderable advantage in her favour towards gaining
this end.

Alice Alington, Margaret's step-sister,[1] had
written her a letter informing her of the steps she
had taken in an effort to win Chancellor Audley's
good offices on their father's behalf. The Chancellor had said he would do for him all that he
would do for his own father, but he thought him
very obstinate, considering that everyone else had
signed, 'save only the blind bishop[2] and he'. And
he told her two fables in answer; but 'In good faith',
she wrote, 'they pleased me nothing, nor did I know
what to say, for I was abashed at his answer.' She
felt that only God could help them now.

Margaret's reply to this letter is interesting and
important from many points of view. The style and
matter seem to suggest that it was written by father
and daughter together, with a good deal of dictation
from the father. Its purpose is clear, he wishes his
motives to be correctly understood. At the same
time it gives a vivid picture of the intimate re-
lationship between them and their lively repartee,
of their intense humanity no less than their deep
spirituality. How closely Margaret watched him
when she gave him Alice's letter to read; she saw

[1] The daughter of More's second wife by her previous
marriage.
[2] John Fisher of Rochester.

him read it to the end, and then, without a word, turn back to the beginning and read it through once again, taking his time over it and giving it his fullest attention, for 'he noted every word', she says. And even when he had come to the end for the second time, still he paused before speaking his mind. His first reaction was one of gratitude and love for the step-daughter who was as dear to him as any of his own children.

As the letter is so long the fables, or allegories, have been omitted. Margaret begins:

When I came next unto my father, I thought it both convenient and necessary to show him your letter,—convenient, that he might thereby see your loving labour taken for him; necessary, that he might see thereby that if he stand still in this scruple of his conscience, (as it is called by many that are his friends, and his wife) all his friends that seem most able to do him good, will either finally forsake him, or peradventure not be able to do him any good at all.

And for these causes, at my next being with him after your letter received, when I had talked with him for a while, first of his diseases both in his breast of old and his reins now, by reason of gravel and stone, and of the cramp also that divers nights grips him in the legs; and that I found by his words that they were not much increased, but continued after their manner was before, sometimes very sore and sometimes less, and that at that time I found him out of pain; and as one in his case might, meetly well-minded, after our

seven psalms and the litany said, to sit and talk and
be merry, beginning first with other things: of the
good comfort of my mother, and the good order of
my brother, and all my sisters, disposing themselves
every day more and more to set little by the world,
and draw more and more to God; and that his household, his neighbours and other good friends abroad
diligently remembered him in their prayers, I added
unto this: I pray, good father, that their prayers and
ours, and your own therewith, may purchase of God
the grace that you may in this great matter, (for which
you stand in this trouble, and for your trouble all we
also that love you), take such a way by time as, standing with the pleasure of God, may content and please
the King, whom you have always found so singularly
gracious unto you, that if you should stiffly refuse to do
the thing that were his pleasure, which, not displeas-
ing God you might do, (as many great, wise and well-
learned men say that in this thing you may), it would
both be a great blot on your name in every wise man's
opinion, and as I myself have heard some say, (whom
you yourself have always taken for well-learned and
good), a peril unto your soul also. But as for that point,
father, I will not be bold to dispute upon, since I trust
in God and your good mind, that you will look surely
thereto. And your learning I know for such that I
know well you can.

But one thing there is, which I and your other
friends find and perceive abroad, which, if it were but
showed to you, you may peradventure mistake to your
great peril, and hope for less harm than, I fear me

sore, shall be likely to fall to you, (for, as for good, I know well that you look for none in this world). I assure you, father, I have received a letter of late from my sister Alice by which I see well, that if you change not your mind you are likely to lose all those friends that are able to do you any good. Or if you lose not their good wills you will at least lose the effect thereof for any good that they shall be able to do you.

With this my father smiled upon me and said: What, mistress Eve, (as I called you when you first came), has my daughter Alice played the serpent with you, and with a letter set you awork to come tempt your father again, and for the favour that you bear him, labour to make him swear against his conscience, and so send him to the devil?

And after that he looked sadly again, and earnestly said unto me: Daughter Margaret, we two have talked of this thing more than twice or thrice, and the same tale, in effect, that you tell me now, and the same fear too, have you twice told me before, and I have twice answered you too, that in this matter if it were possible for me to do the thing that might content the King's grace, and God therewith not offended, then hath no man taken this oath more gladly than I would do, as he that reckoneth himself more deeply bound unto the King's highness for his most singular bounty, many ways showed and declared, than any of them all beside. But since standing with my conscience I can in no wise do it, and that for the instruction of my conscience in the matter, I have not slightly looked but by many years studied and advisedly considered, and never yet could see nor hear that thing, nor do I think I ever shall, that could induce mine own mind to think otherwise than I do, I have no manner of remedy, but God has given me to that strait that either I must deadly displease him, or abide any worldly harm that he shall, for mine other sins under name of this thing, suffer to fall upon me.

Whereof, (as I before this have told you too), I have, before I came here, not left unthought on nor unconsidered the very most and the uttermost that can by possibility fall on me. And albeit that I know mine own frailty full well, and the natural faintness of mine own heart, yet if I had not trusted that God should give me strength rather to endure all things than offend him by swearing ungodly against mine own conscience, you may be very sure I would not have come here. And since I look, in this matter, only to God it matters little to me that men call it as it please them and say it is no conscience, but only a foolish scruple.

At this word I took a good occasion, and said unto him thus: In good faith, father, for my part I neither do, nor can it become me, either to mistrust your good mind or your learning. But because you speak of that which some call but a scruple, I assure you that you shall see by my sister's letter, that one of the greatest nobles in this realm and a man learned too, and your tender friend and very good special lord, (as I dare say you yourself will think when you know who he is, and as you have right effectually proved him,) accounts your conscience in this matter for a right simple scruple. And you may be sure he says it of a good mind and with reason. For he says that where you say your conscience moves you to do this, all the nobles of the realm, and almost all other men too, go boldly forth with the contrary and stick not thereat, there is only yourself and one other man whom, though he be right good and very well learned too, yet I think that few of those who love you would give you the counsel against all other men to lean to his mind alone.

And with this word I gave him your letter that he might see that my words were not feigned, but spoken from his mouth whom he loved much and esteems highly. Thereupon he read over your letter. And when he came to the end he began it afresh and read it over again. And in the reading he made no manner of haste but considered it leisurely and noted every word.

And after that he paused and then he said: Forsooth, daughter Margaret, I find my daughter Alice such as I have ever found her, and I trust ever shall, as naturally thinking of me as you that are mine own. And I take her verily for mine own too, since I have married her mother, and brought her up from childhood, as I have brought up you, in other things and in learning, both, wherein I thank God she finds now some fruit and brings her own up very virtuously and well, whereof God, I thank him, has sent her good store, our Lord preserve them and send her much joy of them, and my good son her gentle husband too, and have mercy on the soul of mine other good son, her first. I am daily bedesman (and so write her) for them all. In this matter she has behaved like herself, wisely and like a true daughter towards me; and in the end of her letter gives as good counsel as any man (that hath wit) would wish; God give me grace to follow it, and God reward her for it.

Now, daughter Margaret, as for my Lord, I not only think, but have also found that he is undoubtedly my singular good lord. And in mine other business concerning the foolish nun, as my cause was good and clear so was he my good lord therein, and Master Secretary my good master too. For which I shall never cease to be faithful bedesman for them both, and I daily pray for them as I pray for myself. And whensoever it should happen (which I trust God shall never happen) that I be found other than a true man to my prince, let them never favour me, either of them, nor would it become them to do so. But in this matter Meg, to tell the truth between you and me, my Lord's Æsop's fables do not greatly move me. But as his wisdom for his pastime told them to my one daughter, so shall I, for my pastime, answer them to thee, Meg, that art mine other. . . .

. . . It seems that my lord signifies by that similitude that of oversight and folly my scrupulous conscience takes for a great perilous thing towards my soul if I were to swear this oath, whereas his Lordship thinks it but a trifle. And I suppose well, Margaret, as you told me just now, that many more besides think the same, both spiritual and temporal men who for their learning and virtue I myself esteemed not a little. And yet should I suppose this to be true I believe that not every man who so thinks so says. But even if they did, daughter, that would not mean much to me, not even though I should see my Lord of Rochester say the same, and swear the oath himself before me too.

For whereas you told me just now that such as love me would not advise me that against all other men I should lean unto his mind alone, truly daughter, no more do I. For although I truly have him in reverent estimation, such that I reckon no one man in this realm to be in wisdom, learning and long approved virtue, meet to be matched and compared with him, yet that in this matter I was not led by him appears well and plainly, both in that I refused the oath before it was offered to him, and in that also that his lordship was content to have sworn of that oath either somewhat more, or in some other manner than I ever minded to do, (as I perceived since, by you, when you moved me to the same).

Truly, daughter, I never intend (God being my good Lord) to pin my soul to another man's back, not even the best man that I know this day living, for I know not whither he may happen to carry it. There is no man living, of whom while he lives, I may make myself sure. Some may do for favour and some may do for fear and so might they carry my soul a wrong way. And some might happen to frame himself a conscience and think that while he did it for fear, God would forgive it. And some may peradventure think that they will repent and be shriven thereof and that so God will remit it them. And some may peradventure be of the mind that if they say one thing and

hink meanwhile the contrary, God regards more their
eart and their tongue, and that therefore their oath
tands upon what they think and not upon what they
ay, as a woman reasoned once when I think you were
here. But in good faith, Marget, I can use no such
ways in so great a matter; if mine own conscience
allowed me I would not fail to do it though other
men refused, so though others refuse not, I dare not
do it, mine own conscience standing against it.

If I had, as I told you, looked but lightly into the
matter I should have cause to fear; but now I have so
looked into it and for so long that I intend to have at
least no less regard for my soul than did once a poor
honest man of the country that was called Company.

And with this he told me a tale, I think I can scant
tell it you again because it hangs upon some terms and
ceremonies of the law. . . . And when my father had
told me this tale, then he said further thus: I pray you
now, good Margaret, tell me this, would you wish
your poor father, being at least somewhat learned, to
regard less the peril of his soul than did there that
honest unlearned man? I meddle not, you know well,
with the conscience of any man that hath sworn, nor
do I take upon me to be their judge. But now if they
do well what their conscience does not reproach them,
and I, with my conscience to the contrary, should for
good company pass on with them and swear as they
do, when all our souls hereafter shall pass out of this
world and stand in judgement at the bar before the
High Judge, if he judge them to heaven and me to the
devil because I did as they did, not thinking as they

thought, if I should then say (as the good man Company said): Mine old good lords and friends, naming such a lord and such, yes, and some bishops, perhaps among those I love best: I swore because you swore and went the way that you went, do likewise for me now, let me not go alone, if there be any good fellowship with you, some of you come with me.

In truth, Margaret, I may say to you in secret counsel, here between us two, (but let it go no further I beseech you heartily) I find the friendship of this wretched world so fickle, that for any entreaty or prayer that I could make, I think that among them all I should not find one who would for good fellowship go to the devil with me. And then, by God, Margaret, if you think so too it is best I suppose rather than have respect to them, even were they twice as many as they are, to have myself respect to mine own soul.

Surely, father, I said, without any scruple at all you may be bold, I dare say, to swear that. But, father, they that think you should not refuse to swear the thing that you see so many, so good men and so well learned, swear before you, mean not that you should swear to bear them good fellowship, nor to pass with them for good company, but that the credence that you may with reason give to their persons for their aforesaid qualities, should well move you to think the oath such of itself, as every man may well swear without peril of their soul, if their own private conscience to the contrary be not the let;[1] and that you well ought

[1] Hindrance, prevention.

to change your own conscience, and have good cause to, in conforming your own conscience to the conscience of so many others, being such as you know them to be. And since it is also by a law commanded by parliament, they think that you are bound to change and reform your conscience upon the peril of your soul, and conform your own, as I said, unto other men's.

Marry, Margaret, said my father again, for the part that you play, you play it not much amiss. But, Margaret, first, as for the law of the land, though every man being born and inhabiting therein is bound to keep it in every case upon some temporal pain, and in many cases upon pain of God's displeasure too, yet there is no man bound to swear that every law is well made, nor bound upon the pain of God's displeasure to perform any such point of the law as were indeed unlawful. Of which manner kind that there may such happen to be made in any part of Christendom I suppose no man doubts, the general Council of the whole body of Christendom evermore in that point excepting; which, though it may make some things better than others, and some things may grow to that point that by another law they may need to be reformed, yet to institute anything in such wise to God's displeasure such as at the making might not lawfully be performed, the Spirit of God that governs his Church has never yet suffered, nor ever shall hereafter, when his whole Catholic Church is lawfully gathered together in a general Council, as Christ has made plain promises in Scripture.

Now if it so happen that in any particular part of Christendom a law be made such that for some part thereof some men think that the law of God cannot bear it, and some others think yes, the thing being in question in such a manner that through divers quarters of Christendom, some that are good men and skilful, both of our own days, and before our days, think some one way; and some others of like learning and goodness think the contrary, in this case he who thinks against the law may neither swear that the law was lawfully made against his own conscience, nor is he bound upon pain of God's displeasure to change his own conscience therein for any particular law made anywhere, other than that of a general Council, or by general faith grown by the working of God universally through all Christian nations; no other authority except one of these two (except a special revelation and express commandment of God) since the contrary opinions of good men and well learned, as I put you the case, made the understanding of the Scriptures doubtful, I can see none that lawfully may command and compel any man to change his own opinion and transfer his own conscience from one side to the other.

For an example of some such manner of things, I have, I am sure, before this time, told you that whether our blessed Lady were conceived in original sin or not, was sometime in great question among the great learned men of Christendom. And whether it is yet decided and determined by any general Council I remember not. But this I remember well, that notwithstanding that the feast of her Conception was then celebrated in the Church (at least in divers provinces) yet was holy S. Bernard, who, as his manifold books made in honour and praise of our Lady do declare, was of devout affection towards all things resounding to her commendation as any man living, such as he thought might well be verified or allowed. Yet, I say, that holy devout man was against that part of her praise as appears well in an epistle of his wherein he right sore and with great reason argues against it and did not approve of the institution of that feast either. Nor was he alone of that mind, but many other well learned men with him, and right holy men too.

Now was there on the other side the blessed holy bishop Saint Anselm, and not alone he either but many well learned and very virtuous also with him. And they are both holy saints in heaven, and many more that were on the other side. Nor was either side bound to change their opinion for the other side, nor for any provincial Council either. But only after the determination of a well assembled general Council would every man be bound to give credence that way, and conform their own conscience to the determination of the general Council; and then all those who before had held the contrary were for that not to blame, but if before such a decision a man had, against his own conscience, sworn to maintain and defend the other side, he would not fail to offend God very sore.

But marry, if on the other side a man would in a matter take away by himself upon his own judgement alone, or with some few, or with never so many, against an evident truth appearing by the common faith of Christendom, this conscience is very damnable. Yes, or if it be not even so fully plain and evident, yet if he see himself with far the fewer part thinking the one way, against far the greater part of as well learned and as good as those are that affirm the thing that he thinks, thinking and affirming the contrary; and that of such folk as he has no reasonable cause wherefore he should not in that matter suppose that those who say they think against his mind, affirm the thing that they say for no other cause but that they think so indeed, this is of very truth a very good occasion to move him, and yet not to compel him to conform his mind and conscience unto theirs.

But Margaret, for what causes I refuse the oath, that thing (as I have often told you) I will never show you, neither you nor anybody else, except the King's Highness should like to command me. Which if his Grace did, I told you this before and how obediently therein I have said. But assuredly daughter, I have refused it, and do, for more causes than one. And for what causes soever I refuse it of this I am sure, that it is well known that of those that have sworn it some of the best learned, before the oath was given them, had said and plainly affirmed the contrary of some of the things that they have now sworn in the oath, and that upon their truth and their learning and not in haste nor suddenly, but often after trying with great diligence to seek and find out the truth.

That might be father, said I, but they might have seen more since.

I will not, said he, dispute, daughter Margaret, against that, nor misjudge any other man's conscience which lies in their own heart far out of my sight. But this I will say that I never heard myself the cause of their change, by any new thing found by authority, than as far as I perceive they had looked on, and as I supose, very well weighed before. Now of the self same things that they saw before, some seem otherwise to them now than they did before, I am for their sakes the gladder a great deal. But anything that ever I saw before seems to me this day the same as it did before. And therefore, though they may do otherwise than they might, yet, daughter, I may not.

As for such things as some men would perhaps say, that I might with reason the less regard their change for any example of theirs taken to the change of my conscience, because to keep the prince's pleasure and avoid his indignation, the fear of losing their worldly substance with regard to the discomfort of their kindred and friends, might perhaps make some men either swear otherwise than they think, or frame their conscience afresh to think otherwise than they thought; any such opinion as this I will not conceive of them. I have better hope of their goodness than to think of them so. For if such things should have turned them, the same things would have been likely to make me do the same, for in good faith I knew few so faint-hearted as myself.

Therefore will I, Margaret, by my will, think no worse of other folk in the thing that I know not, than I find in myself. But as I know well mine own conscience causes me to refuse the oath, so will I trust in God that according to their conscience they have received it and sworn. But whereas you think, Margaret, that they are so many, more than there are on the other side, that think in this thing as I think, surely for your own comfort, that you should not be anxious, thinking that your father casts himself away like a fool, that he would hazard the loss of his substance and perhaps his body too, without any cause why he should so do for the peril of his soul, but rather put his soul in peril thereby too, to this shall I say to you, Marget, that in some of my causes I nothing doubt at all that, though not in this realm, yet in all Christendom round about, there are well learned men still alive who are not the fewer to think as I do. Besides that you know well that it is possible that some men in this realm too do not think so clearly the contrary as by the oath received they have sworn to say.

Now thus far forth I say for such as are still alive. But let me go now to those that are dead and that are, I trust, in heaven, I am sure that it is not the fewer part of them that all the time while they were alive thought in some of the things the way that I think now. I am also, Margaret, of this thing sure enough, that of those holy doctors and saints who are with God in heaven long ago, as no good Christian man doubts, whose books still today remain here in men's hands, there were some who thought some such things as I think now.

I say not that they all thought so, but surely such

and so many as will well appear by their writing, that
I pray God give me the grace that my soul may follow
theirs.

And yet I show you not all, Margaret, that I have
for myself in that sure discharge of my conscience.
But for the conclusion, daughter Margaret, of all this
matter, as I have often told you, I take not upon me
either to define or dispute in these matters, nor do I
rebuke nor impugn any other man's deeds, nor did I
ever write or so much as speak in any company, any
word of reproach in anything that the parliament had
passed; nor do I meddle with the conscience of any
other man who either thinks, or says he thinks, contrary unto mine.

But as concerning mine own self, for thy comfort
shall I say, daughter, to you, that mine own conscience
in this matter (I damn none other man's) is such, as
may well stand with mine own salvation; of that,
Meg, I am as sure as that God is in heaven. And
therefore as for all the rest, goods, lands and life both
(if the chance should so turn out), since this conscience
is so sure for me I verily trust in God he shall rather
strengthen me to bear the loss than against this conscience to swear and put my soul in peril, since all the
causes that I perceive move other men to the contrary,
seem not such unto me so as to make any change in
my conscience.

When he saw me sit with this very sad, as I promise
you, sister, my heart was full heavy for the peril of his
person—for in faith I fear not for his soul—he smiled
upon me and said: How now, daughter Marget?

c

What now, Mother Eve? Where is your mind now? Sit not musing with some serpent in your breast, upon some new persuasion, to offer father Adam the apple once again.

In good faith, father, said I, I can no further go, but am come to Dulcarnon, (as Cressida says in Chaucer,) even at my wits' end. For since the example of so many wise men cannot in this matter move you, I see not what to say more, unless I try to persuade you with the reason that Master Harry Pattenson[1] made. For he met one day one of our men, and when he had asked where you were, and heard that you were in the Tower still, he became even angry with you and said: Why, what aileth him that he will not swear? Why should he stick at swearing? I have sworn the oath myself. And so I can in good faith go now no further either, after so many wise men, whom you take for no example, but to say like Master Harry: Why should you refuse to swear, father, for I have sworn myself?

At this he laughed and said: That word was like Eve too, for she offered Adam no worse fruit than she had eaten herself.

But yet, father, said I, by my troth, I fear me very sore that this matter will bring you into marvellous heavy trouble. You know well that as I showed you, Master Secretary sent you word as your true friend, to remember that the parliament lasteth yet.

Margaret, said my father, I thank him right heartily. But as I showed you then, again, I left this

[1] Sir Thomas' jester-servant, or household fool.

trouble not unthought on. And albeit I knew well that if they would make a law to do me any harm, that law could never be lawful; but God shall, I trust, keep me in that grace so that concerning my duty to my prince, no man shall do me hurt except if he do me wrong, (and then, as I told you, this is like a riddle, a case in which a man may lose his head and have no harm); and notwithstanding also that I have good hope that God shall never suffer so good and wise a prince to requite in such wise the long service of his true faithful servant, yet since there is nothing impossible to happen, I did not forget in this matter the counsel of Christ in the Gospel, that before I begin to build this castle for the safeguard of mine own soul, I should sit and reckon what the charge would be.

I counted, Marget, assuredly full many a restless night, while my wife slept and thought I had slept too, what peril were possible to befal me, so far forth that I am sure none can come above it. And in devising, daughter, thereupon I had a full heavy heart. But yet I thank our Lord for all that, I never thought to change though the very uttermost should happen to me that my fear ran upon.

No, father, said I, it is not the same to think upon a thing that may be, as to see a thing that shall be, as you should (our Lord save you) if it should so happen. And then should you perhaps think what you do not think now, then perhaps it would be too late.

Too late, daughter Margaret? said my father, I beseech our Lord that if ever I make such a change it may be too late indeed. For well I know the change cannot be good for my soul, that change were it to grow by fear. And therefore I pray God that in this world I never have good of such a change. For so much as I take harm here I shall have at the least the less there when I am gone hence. And if it so were that I should faint and fall and for fear swear hereafter, yet would I wish to take harm by the refusing first, for so should I have the better hope for grace to rise again. And albeit, Marget, that I know well that my sinfulness has been such that I know myself to be worthy that God should let me slip, yet I can only trust in his merciful goodness that as his grace has strengthened me hitherto and made me content in my heart to lose goods, land and life too, rather than swear against my conscience, and has also put in the King's good and gracious mind towards me that as yet he has taken from me nothing but my liberty, wherewith (as help me God) his grace has done me so great good by the spiritual profit that I trust I take thereby, that among all his great benefits heaped upon me so thick, I reckon upon my faith my imprisonment even the very chief. I cannot therefore, I say, mistrust the grace of God, that either he shall conserve and keep the King in that gracious mind still to do me no hurt, or else if his pleasure be that for mine other sins I shall suffer in such a cause in sight as I shall not deserve, his grace shall give me that strength to take it patiently, and peradventure somewhat gladly too, whereby his High Goodness (by the merits of his bitter passion joined thereunto, and far surmounting in merit for me all that I can suffer myself) shall make it serve for release of my pain in purgatory, and over that for increase of some reward in heaven.

Mistrust him, Meg, will I not, though I feel me faint. Yes, and though I should feel my fear even at the point to overthrow me too, yet I shall remember how Saint Peter with a blast of wind began to sink for his faint faith, and shall do as he did, call upon Christ and pray him to help. And then I trust he shall set his holy hand unto me, and in the stormy seas hold me up from drowning. Yes, and if he suffer me to play Saint Peter further, and to fall full to the ground, and swear and forswear too (which our Lord for his tender passion keep me from, and let me lose and never win thereby should it happen); yet after that shall I trust that his goodness shall cast upon me his tender piteous eye, as he did upon Saint Peter, and make me stand up again and confess the truth of my conscience afresh, and abide the shame and the harm here of mine own fault.

And finally, Marget, this I know very well, that without my fault he will not let me be lost. I shall therefore with good hope commit myself wholly to him. And if he suffer me for my faults to perish, yet shall I then serve for a praise of his justice. But in good faith, Meg, I trust that his tender pity shall keep my poor soul safe, and make me commend his mercy.

And therefore, mine own good daughter, never trouble your mind for anything that shall ever happen to me in this world. Nothing can come but that which God wills. And I am very sure that whatsoever that may be, however bad it may appear, it shall indeed be the best.

And with this, my good child, I pray you heartily, you and all your sisters, and my sons too, be comforting and servicable to your good mother my wife. And of your good husbands' minds I have no kind of doubt. Commend me to them all, and to my good daughter Alice, and to all my other friends, sisters, nieces, nephews and allies,[1] and unto all our servants, man woman and child, and all my good neighbours and our acquaintance abroad. And I right heartily pray both you and them to serve God and be merry and rejoice in Him. And if anything happen to me that you would be loth, pray to God for me, but trouble not yourself, as I shall full heartily pray for us all that we may meet together once in heaven where we shall make merry for ever, and never have trouble after.

The following is the last of Margaret's letters to her father that is known to exist. She writes to thank him for his letters, showing him all that they mean to her. She seems at last to have accepted the situation and even to have envisaged the possibility that a final parting by death might be the result of her father's determined stand. She now knows he is a great man and a saint:

Mine own most entirely beloved Father,

I think myself never able to give you sufficient thanks for the inestimable comfort my poor heart

---

[1] Relations by marriage.

eceived in the reading of your most loving and godly
letter, showing me the clear shining brightness of your
soul, the pure temple of the Holy Spirit of God, who,
I doubt not, will perpetually rest in you and you in
him.

Father, if all the world had been given to me, it
would have been a small pleasure, in comparison with
the pleasure I received in the treasure of your letter,
which though it were written with a coal, is worthy in
mine opinion to be written in letters of gold.

Father, what moved them to shut you up again, we
can nothing hear. But surely I conjecture that when
they considered that you were of so temperate a mind,
that you were content to abide there all your life with
such liberty, they thought it never possible to incline
you to their will, except by restraining you from
church, and from the company of my good mother,
your dear wife, and us your children. But, father, this
happening was not strange to you, for I shall not
forget how you told us, when we were with you in the
garden, that these things were like enough to befal
you shortly after.

Father, I have many times rehearsed to mine own
comfort your manner and words you had to us when
we were last with you; for which I trust by the grace
of God to be the better while I live, after the wholesome counsel and fruitful example of living I have
had, good father, of you, whom I pray God give me
grace to follow.

Father, I am sorry I have no longer leisure at this
time to talk with you, the chief comfort of my life; I

trust to have occasion to write again shortly. I trust I have your daily prayer and blessing.

> Your most loving obedient daughter and bedeswoman Margaret Roper, who daily and hourly prays for you in this wise, that our Lord of his infinite mercy give you of his heavenly comfort and so assist you with his grace that you never decline in anything from his blessed will, but live and die his true obedient servant. Amen.

# LETTER IV

## TO Margaret Roper

Sir Thomas' reply is a long one. Recounting another interrogation by Cromwell and 'the lords of the Council', he reiterates his right to hold his peace without its being held against him as a vicious act or mere stubborn obstinacy—he is sufficiently well-known for that to be ruled out.

Margaret has now faced the thought of his death. Seeing this, and in preparation for it, her father is at pains to press the possibility home to her in his own inimitable fashion.

More than once he admits his own frailty, for in preparing himself and thinking these things through to the end, his flesh shrank from the pain and ignominy involved. Here he lets his daughter see him in all the loneliness of his steadfast soul.

(The two passages omitted in this letter are repetitions from a previous letter.)

The Holy Spirit of God be with you.

If I would with my writing, mine own good daughter, declare how much pleasure and comfort your daughterly loving letters were unto me, a peck of coals would not suffice to make me the pens. And other pens have I, good Margaret, none here; and therefore can I write you no long process, nor dare I venture, good daughter, to write often.

The cause of my being shut up again did of likelihood grow from my negligent[1] and very plain true word which you remember. And verily as my mind gave me, as I told you in the garden, that some such thing were likely to happen, so doth my mind always give me, that some folk yet ween[2] that I was not so poor as it appeared in the search, and that it may therefore happen, that again soon, oftener than once, some new sudden searches may happen to be made in every house of ours, as narrowly as is possible. Which thing if ever it should so happen can make but game to us who know the truth of my poverty, but if they find out my wife's gay girdle and her golden beads. Howbeit I verily believe in good faith, that the King's grace of his benign pity will take nothing from her.

I thought and yet think, that it may be that I was shut up again, upon some new causeless suspicion, grown peradventure upon some secret sinister information, whereby some folk haply thought that there should be found out against me some other greater things. But I thank our

---

[1] Negligent here means neglectful of the consequences, not irresponsible.

[2] Think, fancy.

Lord whensoever this conjecture hath fallen in
my mind, the clearness of my conscience hath
made my heart hop for joy. For one thing I am
very sure of until now, and trust in God's mercy
to be while I live, that as I have often said unto
you, I shall never harm my prince so long as I do
no wrong in the sight of God, however it may
seem in the sight of men. For to the world wrong
may seem right, sometimes by false conjecturing,
sometimes by false witnesses, as that good Lord
said unto you who is I daresay my very good lord
in his mind, and said it of very good will.

Before the world also, my refusing of this oath
is accounted a criminal offence, and my religious
fear towards God is called obstinacy towards my
Prince. But my Lords of the Council before whom
I refused it might well perceive by the heaviness
of my heart appearing well more ways than one
unto them, that all sturdy stubbornness, whereof
obstinacy groweth, was very far from my mind . . .

And now you see well, Margaret, that it is no
obstinacy to leave the causes undeclared while I
could not declare them without peril. But now it
is accounted great obstinacy that I refuse the oath,
whatsoever my causes be, considering that of so
many wiser and better men none sticked thereat.
. . . Now I have heard since that some say that
this obstinate manner of mine in still refusing
the oath shall peradventure force and drive the
King's Grace to make a further law for me. I
cannot prevent such a law from being made, but

I am very sure that if I died by such a law, I should die for that point innocent before God. And albeit (good daughter) that I think our Lord that hath the hearts of Kings in his hand would never suffer of his high goodness, so gracious a Prince, and so many honourable men, and so many good men as be in the Parliament to make such an unlawful law, as that should be if it so happened, yet lest I note that point unthought upon, but many times more than one revolved and cast in my mind before my coming hither, both that peril and all other that might put my body in peril of death by the refusing of this oath. In devising whereupon, albeit (mine own good daughter) that I found myself (I cry God mercy) very sensitive and my flesh much more shrinking from pain and from death than I thought it the part of a faithful Christian man to be, in such a case as my conscience gave me, that in the saving of my body should stand the loss of my soul; yet I thank our Lord that in that conflict the spirit had in conclusion the mastery, and reason with the help of faith finally concluded that to be put to death wrongfully for doing well (as I am very sure I do in refusing to swear against mine own conscience, being such as I am not upon peril of my soul bound to change whether my death should come without law, or by colour of a law) it is a case in which a man may lose his head and have no harm, but instead of harm inestimable good at the hand of God.

And I thank our Lord (Megge) since I am come hither I set by death every day less than the one before. For though a man lose some of his years in this world, it is more than manifold recompensed by coming the sooner to heaven. And though it be a pain to die while a man is in health, yet I see very few that in sickness die with ease.

And finally, I am very sure that whensoever the time shall come that may happen to come, God knows how soon, in which I should lie sick in my death bed by nature, I shall then think that God had done much for me if he had suffered me to die before by the colour of such a law. And therefore my reason shows me (Margaret) that it were great folly for me to be sorry to come to that death which I would after wish that I had died.

Besides that, a man may happen with less thank of God and more peril of his soul to die as violently and as painfully by many other chances as by enemies or thieves. And therefore, mine own good daughter, I assure you (thanks be to God) the thinking of any such, though it did grieve me before, now grieves me no longer. And yet I know well for all this mine own frailty, and that Saint Peter who feared it much less than I, fell in such fear soon after, that at the word of a simple girl he forsook and forswore our Saviour. And therefore I am not (Megge) so mad as to warrant myself to stand. But I shall pray, and I pray thee, mine own good daughter, to pray with me that it may

please God who hath given me this mind, to give
me the grace to keep it.

And thus have I, mine own good daughter,
disclosed unto you the very secret bottom of my
mind, referring the order thereof only to the
goodness of God, and that so fully that I assure
you Margaret on my faith I never have prayed
God to bring me hence nor deliver me from death,
but referring all things wholly unto his only
pleasure, as to him that seeth better what is best
for me than I do myself.

Nor since I came here did I ever long to set
my foot in mine own house for any desire of, or
pleasure in, my house, but gladly would I sometimes have some talk with my friends, and specially
my wife and you that pertain to my charge. But
since God disposes otherwise I commit all wholly
to his goodness and take daily great comfort in
that I perceive that you live together so charitably
and so quietly; I beseech our Lord to continue it.

And thus, mine own good daughter, putting
you finally in remembrance that if the necessity
should so require, I thank our Lord in this quiet
and comfort is mine heart this day, and I trust in
God's goodness I shall have the grace so to continue, yet (as I said before) I verily trust that God
shall so inspire and govern the King's heart that
he shall not suffer his noble heart and courage to
requite my true faithful heart and service with
such extreme unlawful and uncharitable dealing,
only for the displeasure that I cannot think the

same as others do. But his true subject will I live
and die, and truly pray for him will I, both here
and in the other world too.

And thus mine own good daughter have me
recommended to my good bedfellow and all my
children, men, women and all, with all your babes
and your nurses and all the maids and servants
and all our kin, and all our other friends abroad.
And I beseech our Lord to save them all and keep
them. And I pray you all pray for me, and I shall
pray for you all. And take no thought for me
whatsoever you shall happen to hear, but be merry
in God.

Your tender loving father,

Thomas More, Knight.

# LETTER V

## TO Margaret Roper

This letter is again a reply to one from Margaret. Although Margaret's letter has not been preserved, it is possible to gain a glimpse of its trend by the few lines which Sir Thomas quotes from it with such loving approval:

The Holy Spirit of God be with you.

Your daughterly loving letter, my dearly beloved child, was and is, I faithfully assure you, much more inward comfort unto me than my pen can well express to you, for divers things that I marked therein; but of all things most especially that God of his high goodness giveth you the grace to consider the incomparable difference between the wretched state of this present life, and the wealthy state of the life to come, for them that die in God; and to pray God in such a good Christian fashion, that it may please him—it doth me good here to rehearse your own words—of his tender pity so firmly to rest our love in him, with little regard of this world, and so to flee sin and

embrace virtue, that we may say with St Paul:
For me to live is Christ and to die is gain; and
this: I desire to depart and to be with Christ.[1]

I beseech our Lord, my dearly beloved
daughter, this wholesome prayer that he hath put
in your mind, that it may please him to give your
father the grace daily to remember and pray, and
yourself as you have written it, even so daily
devoutly to kneel and pray it. For surely if God
give us that, he giveth us, and will give us therewith, all that ever we can well wish. And therefore good Marget, when you pray it, pray it for
us both, and I shall on my part do the like, in such
a manner that it shall please our Lord to give me,
poor wretch, that as in this wretched world I have
been very glad of your company and you of mine,
and still would be if we could—as natural charity
bindeth the father and the child—so we may
rejoice and enjoy each other's company, with
our kinsfolk, allies[2] and friends, everlastingly in
the glorious bliss of heaven; and in the meantime,
with good counsel and prayer, each help the other
thitherward.

And where you write these words of your self:
. . . Good father, strengthen my frailty with your
devout prayers. The Father of heaven must
strengthen thy frailty, my good daughter, and the
frailty of thy frail father too. And let us not doubt
but he so will, if we will not be slack in calling

[1] Philippians 1:21 and 23.
[2] Relatives by marriage.

upon him. Of my poor prayers such as they be, you may be bold to reckon. . . . And of yours I put as little doubt. That you fear your own frailty Marget, does not displease me. May God give us both the grace to despair of our own selves and wholly to depend and hang upon the hope and strength of God.

Surely Meg a fainter heart than thy frail father hath, canst thou not have. And yet I verily trust in the great mercy of God, that he shall of his goodness so stay me with his holy hand, that he shall not finally suffer me to fall wretchedly from his favour. And the like trust, dear daughter, I verily conceive of you. And so much the more in that if we call his benefits to mind and often give him thanks for them, we may find many tokens to give us good hope, in spite of all our manifold offences towards him, that, if we will heartily call for it, his great mercy will not be withdrawn from us.

And truly my dear daughter, in this is my great comfort, that albeit I am of nature so shrinking from pain, that I am almost afraid of a fillip, yet in all the agonies that I have had, of which before my coming here, as I have showed you before, I have had neither small nor few, with a heavy fearful heart, forecasting all such perils and painful deaths, as by any manner of possibility might later befal me; and in such thought often lying long restless and wakeful, while my wife thought I had slept, yet in any such fear and heavy pensiveness

—I thank the mighty mercy of God—I never in my mind intended to consent to do anything, even though it mean enduring the uttermost, that in mine own conscience would damnably cast me in the displeasure of God.

It is now, my good daughter, late. And therefore I thus commend you to the Holy Trinity, to guide you, comfort you, and direct you with his Holy Spirit, and all yours, and my wife with all my children and all our other friends.

Thomas More, Knight.

# LETTER VI

## TO Margaret Roper

This letter was written on 2 or 3 May 1535, when
a full year of his imprisonment had been com-
pleted. A day or two before, three Carthusian
Priors and Richard Reynolds a Brigittine monk
and close friend of Sir Thomas, had been brought
to trial and condemned for refusing to take the
oath of Supremacy. Sir Thomas writes to his
daughter in case she had heard this news and
become alarmed about her father, especially as she
may have learnt that he himself had been interrogated on 30 April:

Our Lord bless you.

My dearly beloved daughter,

I doubt not but by reason of the King's Coun-
cillors resorting hither, at this time when—our
Lord be their comfort—these Fathers of the
Charterhouse and Master Reynolds of Sion be
now judged to death for treason, whose matters
and causes I know not, may happen to put you in
trouble and fear of mind concerning me being

here prisoner, specially because it is not unlikely
that you have heard that I also was brought before the Council here myself. I have thought it
necessary to advertise you of the very truth, to the
end that you neither conceive more hope than the
matter giveth, lest upon another turn it might
aggravate your heaviness; nor more grief and fear
than the matter giveth, on the other side.

Wherefore shortly you shall understand that on
Friday the last day of April in the afternoon,
Master Lieutenant came in here unto me and
showed me that Master Secretary wished to speak
with me. Whereupon I shifted my gown and went
out with Master Lieutenant into the gallery to
him. Where I met many, some known and some
unknown, on the way. And coming into the
chamber where his Mastership sat with Master
Attorney, Master Solicitor, Master Bedill, and
Master Doctor Tregonnell, I was offered to sit
with them, which in no wise I would.

Whereupon Master Secretary showed me that
he doubted not but that I had, by such friends as
had been here to see me, been shown the new
statutes made at the last sitting of the Parliament.
Whereunto I answered: Yea verily. Howbeit for
as much as being here I have no conversation with
any people, I thought it little need for me to be-
stow much time upon them, and therefore I re-
delivered the book shortly and the effect of the
statutes I never marked nor studied to put in
remembrance.

Then he asked me whether I had not read the first statute of them, of the King being Head of the Church. Whereunto I answered, Yes. Then his Mastership declared unto me that since it was now by act of Parliament ordained that his Highness and his heirs be, and ever rightfully have been, and perpetually should be Supreme Head on earth of the Church of England under Christ, the King's pleasure was that those of his Council there assembled should demand mine opinion, and what my mind was therein.

Whereunto I answered that in good faith I had well trusted that the King's Highness would never have commanded any such question to be demanded of me, considering that from the beginning I always declared well and truly from time to time my mind unto his Highness, and since that time I had (I said) unto your Mastership Master Secretary also, both by mouth and by writing. And now I have in good faith discharged my mind of all such matters, and neither will dispute King's titles nor Pope's, but the King's true faithful subject I am and will be, and daily I pray for him and for all his, and for you all that are of his honourable Council, and for all the realm, and otherwise than thus I never intend to meddle.

Whereunto Master Secretary answered that he thought this manner of answer would not satisfy nor content the King's Highness, but that his Grace would exact a more full answer. And his Mastership added thereunto that the King's High-

ness was a prince not of rigour but of mercy and
pity, and though he had found obstinacy at some
time in any of his subjects, yet when he should
find them at another time conformable and submit
themselves his Grace would show mercy. And that
concerning myself his Highness would be glad to
see me take such conformable ways so that I
might be abroad again among other men as I have
been before.

Whereunto I shortly answered (after the inward
affection of my mind) that for a very truth I would
never meddle in the world again, to have the
world given me. And to the rest of the matter I
answered in effect as before, showing that I had
fully determined with myself neither to study nor
meddle with any matter of this world, but that my
whole study should be upon the passion of Christ
and mine own passage out of this world.

Upon this I was commanded to go forth for a
while, and was after called in again. At which
time Master Secretary said unto me that though
I was prisoner and condemned to perpetual prison,
yet I was not thereby discharged of mine obedience and allegiance unto the King's Highness.
And thereupon demanded me whether I thought
that the King's Grace might exact of me such
things as are contained in the statutes, and upon
like punishment as he might of other men. Whereto I answered that I would not say the contrary.
Whereto he said that likewise as the King's Highness would be gracious to them that he found

conformable, so his Grace would follow the course of his laws towards such as he shall find obstinate. And his Mastership said further that my demeanour in that matter was a thing likely to make other men be as obstinate as they are.

Whereto I answered that I give no man occasion to hold any point one way or the other, nor ever gave any man advice or counsel therein one way or the other. And for conclusion I could no further go whatsoever pain should come thereof. I am, said I, the King's true faithful subject and daily bedesman and pray for his Highness and all his and all the realm. I do nobody harm, I say harm of none, I think harm of none but wish everybody good. And if this be not enough to keep a man alive, in good faith I long not to live. And I am dying already, and have since I came here been divers times in the case that I thought to die within one hour, and I thank our Lord I was never sorry for it, but rather sorry when I saw the pang past. And therefore my poor body is at the King's pleasure—would God my death might do him good.

After this Master Secretary said: Well, you find no fault in that statute, find you any in any of the other statutes after? Whereto I answered: Sir, whatsoever thing should seem to me other than good in any of the statutes, or in that statute either, I would not declare what fault I found, nor speak thereof.

Whereunto his Mastership said full gently that

of anything that I had spoken no advantage should
be taken; and whether he said further that there
was none to be taken, I am not well remembered.
But he said that report should be made unto the
King's Highness, and his gracious pleasure known.

Whereupon I was delivered again to Master
Lieutenant, who was then called in, and so I was
by Master Lieutenant brought again into my
chamber, and here I am still in such case as I
was, neither better nor worse.

That which is to follow lieth in the hand of
God, whom I beseech to put in the King's mind
whatever is his high pleasure, and in mine to mind
only the weal of my soul, with little regard of my
body. And you with all yours, and my wife, and
all my children, and all our friends both bodily
and spiritually well to fare. And I pray you and
them all pray for me, and take no thought whatsoever shall happen to me. For I verily trust in
the goodness of God, seem it never so evil in this
world, it shall indeed in another world be for the
best.

> Your loving father,
> Thomas More, Knight.

Sir Thomas was not deceived by Cromwell's speaking to him 'full gently' and promising that no
advantage would be taken of all he had said, for
Roper tells us what he did, once back in his cell:

'As soon as Master Secretary was gone, to express what comfort he received of his words, he

wrote with a coal, for ink he had none, this
verse:

> Eye-flattering Fortune, look thou ne'er so fair,
> Or ne'er so pleasantly begin to smile,
> As though thou wouldst my ruin all repair,
> During my life thou shalt not me beguile:
> Trust shall I God, to enter in awhile
> Thy haven of heaven sure and uniform,
> E'er after thy calm look I for a storm.'

A few days after the above letter was written,
Margaret was with her father, and as they looked
out of his small window they saw the Carthusians
being brought out for execution. Turning to Margaret standing there beside him, he said somewhat
wistfully: 'Lo, dost thou not see, Meg, that these
blessed fathers be now as cheerfully going to their
deaths as bridegrooms to their marriage? Whereas
thy silly father, Meg, God thinking him not worthy
so soon to come to that eternal felicity, leaveth him
here yet still in the world, further to be plagued
and turmoiled with misery.'

# LETTER VII

## TO Margaret Roper

Sir Thomas was interrogated again on 3 June, and for the last time he wrote a long account of it to his beloved daughter. His health was failing rapidly and he was very weary of the long-drawn-out war of attrition.

Our Lord bless you and all yours.

Forasmuch, dearly beloved daughter, as it is likely that you either have heard, or shortly shall hear, that the Council was here this day, and that I was before them, I have thought it necessary to send you word how the matter stands. And verily to be short, I perceive little difference between this time and the last. For as far as I can see, the whole purpose is, either to drive me to say precisely the one way, or else precisely the other.

Here sat my Lord of Canterbury, my Lord Chancellor, my Lord of Suffolk, my Lord of Wiltshire and Master Secretary. After my coming in, Master Secretary rehearsed in what way he had reported unto the King's Highness, what had been said by his Grace's Council to me, and what had been answered by me to them at my being before them last. Which thing his Mastership rehearsed in good faith very well as I acknowledged and confessed and heartily thanked him for it.

Whereupon he added thereunto that the King's Highness was not at all content or satisfied with mine answer, but thought that by my conduct I had been the occasion of much bad influence and harm in the realm, and that I had an obstinate mind and an evil one towards him, and that my duty was to be his subject, and so he had sent them now in his name to command me upon my allegiance to make a plain and determinate answer, as to whether I thought the statute lawful or not, and that I should either acknowledge and confess it lawful that his Highness should be Supreme Head of the Church in England, or else to utter plainly my malignity.

Whereto I answered that I had no malignity and therefore I could utter none. And as to the matter I could make no other answer than I had made before, which answer his Mastership had there rehearsed. Very heavy I was that the King's Highness should have any such opinion of me. Howbeit, if there were one who had informed his Highness many evil things of me that were untrue, to which his Highness for the time gave credence, I would be very sorry that he should have that opinion of me even for the space of one day. Howbeit, if I were sure that another should come on the morrow by whom his Grace should know the truth of mine innocence, I should in the meanwhile comfort myself with the consideration of that. And in like wise now, though it be great heaviness to me that his Highness have such an opinion of me for the while, yet have I no remedy to help it, but only to comfort myself with this consideration, that I know very well that the time shall come when God shall declare my truth towards his Grace before him and all the world.

And whereas it might haply seem to be but small cause for comfort because I might take harm here first in the meanwhile, I thanked God that my case was such in this matter through the clearness of mine own conscience, that though I might have pain I could not have harm, for a man may in such a case lose his head and have no harm. For I was very sure that I had no corrupt affection, but that I had always from the beginning truly accustomed myself to look first upon God and next upon the King, according to the lesson that his Highness taught me at my first coming to his noble service, the most virtuous lesson that ever prince taught his servant; whose Highness to have of me such an opinion is my great heaviness, but I have no means, as I said, to help it, but only comfort myself in the meantime with the hope of that joyful day in which my truth towards him shall be well known. And in this matter I could not go further, nor could I make any other answer.

To this it was said by my Lord Chancellor and

Master Secretary both, that the King might by his laws compel me to make a plain answer thereto, either the one way or the other. Whereunto I answered I would not dispute the King's authority, what his Highness might do in such a case, but I said that verily under correction it seemed to me somewhat hard. For if it so were that my conscience put me against the statutes (wherein how my mind gives me I make no declaration), then I nothing doing and nothing saying against the statute, it were a very hard thing to compel me to say either precisely with it against my conscience to the loss of my soul, or precisely against it to the destruction of my body.

To this Master Secretary said that I had before this, when I was Chancellor, examined heretics and thieves and other malefactors, and gave me great praise above my deserving in that behalf. And he said that I then, as he thought and as the least wise Bishops did use to examine heretics, whether they believed the Pope to be head of the Church and used to compel them to make a precise answer thereto. And why should not then the King, since it is a law made here that his Grace is Head of the Church, here compel men to answer precisely to the law here as they did then concerning the Pope.

I answered and said that I protested that I intended not to defend any part or stand in dispute, but I said there was a difference between those two cases, because at that time, as well here

as elsewhere throughout Christendom the Pope's
power was recognised for an undoubted thing, and
not like a thing agreed in this realm and the contrary taken for truth in other realms. Whereunto
Master Secretary answered that they were as well
burned for the denying of that as they be beheaded
for the denying of this, and therefore as good
reason to compel them to make precise answer to
the one as to the other.

Whereto I answered that since in this case a
man is not by law of one realm so bound in his
conscience, where there is a law of the whole body
of Christendom to the contrary in matter touching belief, as he is by law of the whole body
though there happen to be made in some place
a local law to the contrary, the reasonableness or
the unreasonableness in binding a man to a precise answer standeth not in the respect or difference between beheading or burning, but because
of the difference in charge of conscience, the
difference standeth between beheading and hell.

Much was there answered to this both by
Master Secretary and my Lord Chancellor, too
long to rehearse. And in conclusion they offered
me an oath by which I should be sworn to make
a true answer to such things as should be asked
me on the King's behalf, concerning the King's
own person.

Whereto I answered that verily I never pur-
posed to swear any book oath more while I lived.
Then they said that was very obstinate if I would

refuse that, for every man doth it in the Star Chamber and everywhere. I said that was true but I had not so little foresight but that I might well conjecture what could be part of my interrogation and it was as good to refuse it at first, as afterwards.

Whereto my Lord Chancellor answered that he thought I guessed truth, for I should see them and so they were showed me, and they were but two.[1] The first whether I had seen the statute. The other whether I believed that it were a lawfully made interrogation or not. Whereupon I refused the oath and said further by mouth that the first I had before confessed, and to the second I would make no answer.

This was the end of the communication and I was thereupon sent away. In the communication before, it was said that it was marveled that I persisted so much in my conscience while at the utmost I was not sure of it. Whereto I said that I was very sure that mine own conscience so informed as it is by such diligence as I have so long taken therein, may stand with mine own salvation. I meddle not with the conscience of those that think otherwise, every man *suo domino stat et cadit*.[2] I am no man's judge.

It was also said unto me that if I had as well be out of the world as in it, as I had said, why did I not speak out plainly against the statute. It

[1] The questions put to him on the King's behalf.
[2] 'Stands or falls before his own master.' (Romans 14:4.)

appeared well I was not content to die though I
said so. Whereto I answered as the truth is, that
I have not been a man of such holy living that I
might be bold to offer myself to death, lest God
for my presumption might suffer me to fall, and
therefore I put not myself forward, but draw back.
Howbeit if God draw me to it himself, then I trust
in his great mercy that he will not fail to give me
grace and strength.

In conclusion Master Secretary said that he
liked me this day much worse than he did the last
time. For then, he said, he pitied me much, but
now he thought I meant not well. But God and
I know both, that I mean well, and so I pray God
do by me.

I pray you be, you and mine other good friends,
of good cheer whatsoever befal me, and take no
thought for me but pray for me as I do and shall
do for you and all them.

Your tender loving father,<br>
Thomas More, Knight.

The final interrogation was on 14 June, and a fortnight later he was brought to trial.

D

# LETTER VIII

## TO MARGARET ROPER

On 1 July Sir Thomas was taken by boat to stand his trial at the bar of the Court of King's Bench, in Westminster Hall. After the long indictment had been read, and he had made his defence, it took the jury no more than fifteen minutes to return the verdict of guilty. Sentence of death was pronounced by the Lord Chancellor—and the tragic farce was over.

He was then taken back to the Tower by the same way, but this time with the edge of the executioner's axe pointing towards the prisoner. Tipstaves went before him, carrying their silver-tipped staves, these were the officers who had to lead the accused from the court into custody. On either side of him marched the halberdiers shouldering their long-handled, spear-pointed battle-axes.

In his perfect little biography of his father-in-law, Margaret's husband Will Roper tells of the daughter's last meeting with her dearly-loved father—how she waited about the Tower wharf where she knew he would have to pass on his return

journey. As soon as she saw him coming she ran to
him, pressing her way through the crowds and
through the armed guard surrounding him, and
after kneeling for his blessing, openly threw her
arms round his neck and kissed him fondly; how
he gave her his blessing and comforted her, showing his pleasure at seeing her unashamed affection
for him. Then she drew back to allow him to pass
on, but suddenly, probably before she knew she had
done it, she was back in his arms, kissing him over
and over again, unable to let him go; all she could
say was: 'Oh, father, father!', while the silent
crowd wept.

During the next four days before his execution
he saw none of his family, and on 5 July he wrote
his last letter to Margaret, his final farewell to all
his dear ones. It is a most precious and moving
letter, where he tries to remember each single person of his family and household. It gives the im-
pression of having been written hastily, and is, in
fact, unfinished. As usual it is written with a piece
of charcoal:

Our Lord bless you, good daughter, and your good
husband, and your little boy,[1] and all yours and
all my children, and all my god-children and all
our friends. Recommend me when you may to my
good daughter Cecily,[2] whom I beseech our Lord

[1] Her third child, Thomas, born 1534.
[2] His third daughter. His children were Margaret, Elizabeth, Cecily, John.

to comfort. And I send her my blessing, and to all her children, and pray her to pray for me. I send her a handkerchief; and God comfort my good son her husband.[1] My good daughter Daunce[2] hath the picture in parchment that you delivered me from my Lady Coniers,[3] her name is on the backside. Show her that I heartily pray her that you may send it in my name to her again, for a token from me to pray for me.

I like specially well Dorothy Coly,[4] I pray you be good unto her. I should like to know whether this be she that you wrote me of. If not, yet I pray you be good to the other as you may in her affliction, and to my good daughter Joan Aleyn too.[5] Give her, I pray you, some kind answer, for she sued hither to me this day to pray you be good to her.

I cumber you, good Margaret much, but I would be sorry if it should be any longer than tomorrow, for it is St Thomas' even[6] and the utas[7] of St Peter; and therefore tomorrow long I to go

---

[1] Giles Heron.

[2] His daughter Elizabeth who married W. Daunce on the same day as her sister Cecily married Giles Heron, More's ward.

[3] Nothing is known of her.

[4] Margaret's maid; married John Harris, More's secretary. It was they who preserved so many of More's letters until they were in tatters and hardly readable, then they inked them over to preserve them.

[5] Another maid.

[6] Eve of the translation of the relics of St Thomas à Beckett.

[7] Octave day of the feast of Sts Peter and Paul.

o God, it were a day very meet and convenient
or me.

I never liked your manner towards me better
han when you kissed me last, for I love when
daughterly love and dear charity hath no leisure
to look to worldly courtesy.

Farewell, my dear child, and pray for me, and
I shall for you and all your friends, that we may
merrily meet in heaven. I thank you for your great
cost.

I send now unto my good daughter Clement[1]
her algorism stone,[2] and I send her and my good
son[3] and all hers God's blessing and mine.

I pray you at time convenient recommend me
to my good son John More. I liked well his natural
fashion.[4] Our Lord bless him and his good
wife my loving daughter,[5] to whom I pray him
be good, as he hath great cause; and that if the
land of mine come into his hand, he break not
my will concerning his sister Daunce. And our
Lord bless Thomas and Austin[6] and all that they
shall have.

---

[1] Margaret Gigs, wife of John Clement.
[2] Probably a slate for calculation.
[3] John Clement.
[4] John More had also publicly asked his father's blessing
when he came from judgement.
[5] Ann Cresacre.
[6] Children of John More. Thomas was born in 1533 and
died in 1606, having had to suffer all his life the penalties
exacted from Catholic recusants. His youngest son was
Cresacre More, father of Helen More, foundress of the
Benedictine Dames of Cambrai, now at Stanbrook Abbey.

Soon after dawn the next morning, Tuesday 6 July
a Tower official came in to Sir Thomas with the
message from the King and Council that he was to
suffer death before nine of the clock that same
morning. The King also required him not to use
many words at the last. To this he replied that he
was glad of the warning because he had intended
to speak, 'but of no matter wherewith his Grace or
any other should have cause to be offended. Never-
theless whatsoever I intended, I am ready obediently to conform myself to his Grace's commandment.'

Then he asked that his daughter might be
allowed to be at his burial, and was told that the
King had already granted this, and that his wife
and friends might also be there. The gaoler himself wept as he was leaving the cell, and Sir Thomas
had to comfort him: 'Quiet yourself and be not
discomforted, for I trust that we shall, once in
heaven, see each other full merrily, where we shall
be sure to live and love together in joyful bliss
eternally.'

Then he changed into his best clothes as for a
King's banquet; but when the Lieutenant saw this
he was against it, saying that the executioner who
would claim it was only a common fellow. Sir
Thomas argued that if it were cloth of gold he
would be glad for the fellow to have it who would
be doing him this day 'so singular a benefit'. Only
after some 'importunate persuasion' did he submit
and change again into something less than his best.

But in place of it he took an angel of gold[1] and gave that instead for the executioner's reward.

Then the Lieutenant led him down the dark Tower stairs and out into the bright mid-summer morning. The grass must never have seemed so green to him as they crossed it to the scaffold. The boards had been put up hurriedly and were none too steady. As Thomas put his foot on the first shaky step he asked the Lieutenant to see him safely up, 'and for my coming down', he said, 'let me shift for myself'.

'Then desired he all the people thereabout to pray for him, and to bear witness with him that he should now there suffer death, in and for the faith of the Holy Catholic Church. Which done, he kneeled down, and after his prayers said, turned to the executioner, and with a cheerful countenance spoke thus to him: "Pluck up thy spirits, man, and be not afraid to do thine office; my neck is short, take heed therefore thou strike not awry for saving of thine honesty."

'So passed Sir Thomas More out of this world to God, upon the very same day which he himself had most desired.'[2]

'Tomorrow long I to go to God, it were a day very meet and convenient for me.' 'So passed Sir Thomas More out of this world to God'—a man

---

[1] Angel-noble, an English gold coin.
[2] 'The Life of Sir Thomas More, Knight, sometime Chancellor of England, written by his son-in-law, William Roper, of Eltham in the County of Kent, Esquire.'

who inspired the deepest affection in almost every one who knew him. He combined wit, passion, wisdom, scorn, gentleness and integrity in a degree rarely equalled. He himself had an intense and unalterable affection, warm and generous, which gave to others an anchor of stability in a disintegrating world. He showed in legal matters unbending straightforwardness, combined with skill and patience; caring nothing for public recognition and honours, he simply went his own detached and peaceful way. In one of his best moments Cardinal Wolsey wrote to the King asking for a remuneration for Thomas More 'because he is not the most ready to speak and solicit his own case'.

This great Englishman, and, surely, our greatest Lord Chancellor, with all his underlying seriousness, was almost invariably gay, drawing his companions out of themselves and their sad thoughts with his 'merrily meet in heaven'. Beloved father of a family twice as numerous as the number of his own children, he lived a life of holiness with a devotion that never flagged; deeply immersed in the world's affairs, he was never submerged by them.

## MEDITATIONS AND PRAYERS
## WRITTEN IN PRISON

'I do earnestly pray Almighty God that for
his mercy sake he will bring us from this
wretched and stormy world into his rest,
where we shall need no letters, where no wall
shall dissever us, where no porter shall keep
us from talking together.'

*From Thomas More's last letter to his old
and dear friend Master Anthony Bonvisi*

*A Treatise made in the year of our Lord 1534*
*by Sir Thomas More, Knight,*
*while he was prisoner in the Tower of London*

## TO RECEIVE THE BLESSED BODY
## OF OUR LORD
*Sacramentally and virtually both*

# BEFORE COMMUNION

Such is the wonderful bounty of Almighty God,
that he not only does vouchsafe, but also does
delight to be with men, if they prepare to receive
him with honest and clean souls, whereof he says:
My delight and pleasure are to be with the sons
of men (Prov. 8, 31).

And how can we doubt that God delights to be
with the sons of men when the Son of God, and
very Almighty God himself, liked not only to
become the Son of man, that is to say, the Son
of Adam the first man, but over that, in his innocent manhood to suffer his painful passion for the
redemption and restitution of man.

We must consider well and examine surely
what state our soul stands in, and in this proving

and examination of ourselves, one very special point must be to prove and examine ourself and see that we be in the right faith and belief concerning that holy blessed Sacrament itself; that that is to say, that we verily believe that it is, as indeed it is, under the form and likeness of bread, the very body, flesh and blood of our holy Saviour Christ himself; the very selfsame body and the very selfsame blood that died and was shed upon the cross for our sin, and the third day gloriously did rise again to life, and with the souls of holy saints fetched out of hell, ascended and mounted up wonderfully into heaven, and there sitteth on the right hand of the Father, and shall visibly descend in great glory to judge the living and the dead, and reward all men after their works.

We must, I say, see that we firmly believe that this blessed Sacrament is not a bare sign, or a figure, or a token of that holy body of Christ; but that it is in perpetual remembrance of his bitter passion that he suffered for us, the selfsame precious body of Christ that suffered it by his own almighty power and unspeakable goodness, consecrated and given to us.

And this point of belief is, in the receiving of this blessed Sacrament, of such necessity and such weight with them that have years of discretion, that without it they receive it plainly to their damnation. And that point believed very full and fastly must needs be a great occasion to move any man in all other points to receive it well. For note well the words of St Paul: 'He that eateth of this bread and drinketh of this cup unworthily eateth and drinketh judgement upon himself, in that he discerneth not the body of our Lord' (1 Cor. 11, 29). Lo here this blessed Apostle well declares that he who in any way unworthily receives this most excellent Sacrament, receives it unto his own damnation, in that he well declares by his evil demeanour towards it in his unworthy receiving of it, that he neither discerns it, nor judges it, nor takes it for the very body of our Lord, as indeed it is.

And verily, this point deeply rooted in our breast should set all our heart in a fervour of devotion towards the worthy receiving of that blessed body.

But now, having the full faith of this point fast grounded in our heart, that the thing which we receive is the blessed body of Christ, I trust there shall not greatly need any great information to teach us, or any great exhortation further to stir and excite us, with all humble manner and reverent behaviour to receive him.

For if we will but consider, if there were a great worldly prince who for special favour towards us, were to come and visit us in our house, what a business we would then make, and what a work it would be for us to see that our house were trimmed up in every point, to the best of our possible power, and everything so provided and ordered that he should by his honourable reception, perceive what affection we bear him, and in what high estimation we hold him! We should soon, by the comparing of that worldly prince and this heavenly Prince together—between which two there is far less comparison than there is between a man and a mouse—inform and teach ourself with how lowly a mind, how tender loving a heart, how reverent humble a manner we should endeavour to receive this glorious heavenly King, the King of all kings, almighty God himself, who so lovingly does vouchsafe to enter, not only into our house . . . to which the noble man Centurion acknowledged himself unworthy . . . but his precious body into our vile wretched carcase, and his Holy Spirit into our poor soul.

What diligence can here suffice us? What solicitude can we think here enough against the coming of this almighty King, coming for so special a gracious favour, not to put us to cost, not to spend of ours, but to enrich us of his, and that after so manifold displeasures done him so unkindly by us, against so many of his incomparable benefits before done unto us. How would we now labour and foresee that the house of our soul, into which God is coming to rest, should neither have any poisoned spider or cobweb of deadly sin hanging in the roof, nor so much as a straw, or a feather of any light or vicious thought that we might spy on the floor, but we would wipe it away!

But forasmuch, good Christian readers, as we neither can attain this great point of faith, nor any other virtue but by the special grace of God of whose high goodness every good thing comes, for as St James says: Every good gift, and every perfect gift, is from above, descending from the Father of lights (James 1, 17), let us therefore pray for his gracious help in the attaining of his faith, and for his help in the cleansing of our soul against his coming, that he may make us worthy to receive him worthily. And ever let us of our own part fear our unworthiness, and on his part trust boldly upon his goodness. For if we willingly leave our own endeavour undone upon the trust and comfort of his goodness, then is our hope no hope, but a very foul presumption.

Then when we come unto his holy board, into the presence of his blessed body, let us consider his high glorious majesty which his high goodness there hides from us, and the proper form of his holy flesh covered under the form of bread, both to keep us from abashment, such as we could not perhaps abide, and also for the increase of the merit of our faith in the obedient belief of that thing, at his commandment, whereof our eyes and our reason seem to show us the contrary.

And yet, forasmuch as we believe it, yet many of us believe very faint and far from the point of such vigour and strength as would God we had, let us say unto him with the father that had the dumb son: 'I believe Lord, but help thou my lack of belief' (Mark 9, 23). And with his blessed Apostles: 'Lord, increase faith in us' (Luke 17, 5).

Let us also with the poor Publican, in knowledge of our own unworthiness, say with all meekness of heart: 'Lord God, be merciful to me, sinner that I am' (Luke 18, 13). And with the Centurion: 'Lord, I am not worthy that thou shouldst come into my house' (Matt. 8, 8).

And yet with all this remembrance of our own unworthiness and therefore the great reverence, fear and dread for our own part, let us not forget on the other side to consider his inestimable goodness who dies not disdain, for all our unworthiness, to come unto us and to be received by us.

But likewise as at the sight or receiving of this excellent memorial of his death—for in remembrance thereof does he thus consecrate and give his own blessed flesh and blood to us—we must with tender compassion remember and call to mind the bitter pains of his most painful passion. And yet therewith rejoice and be glad in the consideration of his incomparable kindness, which in his so suffering for us, to our inestimable benefit, he showed and declared towards us. So must we be both sore afraid of our own unworthiness, and yet therewith be right glad and in great hope at the consideration of his unmeasurable goodness.

## AFTER COMMUNION

Now when we have received our Lord and have
him in our body, let us not then let him alone,
getting us forth about other things, looking no
more unto him, but let all our business be about
him. Let us by devout prayer talk to him, by
devout meditation talk with him. Let us say with
the prophet: 'I will hear what our Lord will speak
within me' (Ps 84, 9).

For surely, if we set aside all other things and
attend unto him, he will not fail with good in-
spirations to speak such things to us, within us,
as shall serve to the great spiritual comfort and
profit of our soul. And, therefore, let us with
Martha provide that all our inward business may
be pertaining to him, in making cheer to him, and
to his company for his sake,—that is to say, to
poor folk, of whom he takes every one not only for
his disciple, but also as for himself. For himself
said: 'What you have done to one of the least of
these my brethren, you have done it to myself.'
And let us with Mary also sit in devout meditation and hearken well what our Saviour, being
now our guest, will inwardly say unto us.

Now we have a special time of prayer while he
that made us, he that has bought us, he whom we
have offended, he that shall judge us, he that shall

either damn us or save us, is of his great goodness become our guest and is personally present within us, and that for no other purpose but to be asked for pardon and thereby to save us.

Let us not lose this time therefore, suffer not this occasion to slip, for we can little tell whether we shall ever get it again or never. Let us endeavour ourself to keep him still, and let us say with his two disciples that were going to the castle of Emmaus: 'Tarry with us, good Lord' (Luke 24, 29). And then shall we be sure that he will not go from us but if we unkindly put him from us.

Let us, good Christian readers, receive him in such wise as did the good publican Zaccheus; with such alacrity, with such quickness of spirit, with such gladness and such spiritual rejoicing as this man received our Lord into his house, may our Lord give us the grace to receive his blessed body and blood, his holy soul and his almighty Godhead, both into our bodies and into our souls, that the fruit of our good works may bear witness unto our conscience, that we receive him worthily and in such full faith and such a stable purpose of good living as we be bound to do. And then shall God give us a gracious sentence and say upon our soul, as he said upon Zaccheus: 'This day is health and salvation come unto this house' (Luke 19, 9), which that holy blessed person of Christ, whom we verily receive in the blessed Sacrament, through the merits of his bitter passion vouchsafe, good Christian readers, to grant unto us all.

# ON LOVING ONE'S ENEMY

Bear no malice nor evil will to any man living. For either the man is good or nought. If he be good and I hate him, then I am nought. If he be nought, either he shall amend and die good and go to God, or abide nought and go to the devil.

And then let me remember that if he shall be saved, he shall not fail—if I be saved too, as I trust to be—to love me very heartily and I shall then likewise love him. And why should I now, then, hate one for this while, who shall hereafter love me for evermore? And why should I be now enemy to him with whom I shall in time to come be coupled in eternal friendship?

And on the other side, if he shall continue nought and be damned, then there is so outrageous an eternal sorrow coming to him, that I may well think myself a deadly cruel wretch if I would not now rather pity his pain than malign his person.

If anyone should say that we may well with good conscience wish an evil man harm, lest he should do harm to other folk such as are innocent and good, I will not now dispute upon that point, for this root has more branches to be well weighed and considered than I can now conveniently write, having none other pen than a coal.

But verily thus will I say, that I will give counsel to every good friend of mine, that if he be put in such a position that the punishment of an evil man be in his charge by reason of his office, let him leave the desire of punishing unto God, and unto such other folk as are so grounded in charity and so fast cleave to God, that no secret, shrewd, cruel affection, under cloak of a just and virtuous zeal, can creep in and undermine them.

But let us who are no better than men of a mean sort ever pray for such merciful amendment in other folk as our own conscience shows us that we have need of in ourselves.

*Here follow certain devout and virtuous*
*Instructions Meditations and Prayers*
*made and collected by*
*Sir Thomas More, Knight*
*while he was prisoner in the Tower of London*

## ON THE FEAR OF DEATH

Whosoever so saves his life that he displeases God thereby shall soon after, to his no little grief, full sore mislike the same. For if you save your life you will on the morrow so deadly hate your life that at heart you will be full heavy that the day before you did not lose your life. For you will surely remember that you must certainly die, but how, or how soon, that you know not at all. And just cause have you to fear lest on such delay of death should perhaps follow the everlasting torments of hell, where men shall sore long to die and death shall flee from them (Apoc. 9, 6). Whereas by the enduring of the death which you so much abhor there would undoubtedly have followed the everlasting joys of heaven.

What folly it is then for you to avoid this temporal death so as thereby to fall in peril of purchasing yourself eternal death, and yet therewith not to escape your temporal death, but perhaps for a while only to delay your death.

For put the case that you might for a while avoid the danger of death, are you therefore sure either to continue your life for ever, or at another time to die and feel no pain? Nay, rather it may perchance fare with you as it fared with the rich man that assuredly reckoned himself to live full many a year, to whom Christ said: 'This night, thou fool, shall they bereave thee of thy life' (Luke 12, 20). And again, this are you well assured of, that you will both die once, and also that you cannot live here long, for man's life here passes away so shortly.

Finally, as I suppose, of this you never have the least doubt, that when the time shall come, in which you lie sick on your death-bed, and begin to feel the painful pangs of death so dreadfully drawing on, then will you heartily wish, for the saving of your soul, that you had died many a day before by a sharp and cruel death. Then have you no cause to fear so sore that thing should happen which, as you know right well, you would before long be wishing had befallen you before.

Whosoever suffers any trouble or adversity according to the will of God, must wholly commit his soul into the hands of God, his trusty and faithful Creator. 'Be not discouraged, my well-beloved brethren,' saith St Peter, 'by reason of the extreme persecution that is amongst you, which is sent you for a proof of your patience, as though some strange thing were befallen unto you; but inasmuch as you be partakers of Christ's pains and passion, full heartily rejoice, that you may likewise rejoice at the revelation of his glory' (1 Pet 4, 12).

What a shame it would be then for a Christian man to be content rather to lose the life and bliss everlasting, than suffer a short death somewhat before his time, which he is so well assured he must suffer before long; and unless he repent in time, straight upon his temporal death will he fall into eternal death, and the same so horrible and painful that it far exceedeth all other kinds of death!

If it were possible for a man with his corporal eyes to behold one of those grisly fiends which in so great number daily look and long for us, to torment us for ever in hell, the fear of him alone would make him not regard at all the terrible threats that any man could imagine. And how much less would he regard them, if he might possibly see heaven open and Jesus Christ standing there, as did the blessed St Stephen! (Acts 7, 55).

'Your adversary the devil, saith St Peter, like a roaring lion, runneth about seeking whom he may devour' (1 Pet 5, 8). But hark what St Bernard saith: 'I humbly thank that mighty Lion of the tribe of Juda, well may this lion roar but bite me he cannot. Threaten he us never so much, let us not be such beastly cowards that only for his rude roaring we fall down flat to the ground.'

For a very beast is he, and hath no reason indeed, who is either so feeble spirited that for fear alone giveth over, or so discomforted by a vain imagination of the pains that he may have to suffer, that at the bare blast of the trumpet, before ever the battle begin, he is quite and clean overthrown without any stroke at all.

'You have not resisted as yet to the shedding of your blood' (Hebr. 12, 4), saith that valiant captain who knew right well that the roaring of this lion was nothing to be passed on. And another saith: 'Stand stiff against the devil and he will flee from you' (James 4, 7). Stand stiff, I say, with a strong and steadfast faith, for Isaias giveth us warning before, that they who, having no hope of God's help, fly for succour to man's help, shall both themselves and their helpers with them, come to utter confusion.

# A LITANY OF PETITIONS

The following prayers were written by St Thomas in the upper and lower margins of his prayer book, on eighteen consecutive pages.

Give me thy grace, good Lord, to set the world at
    nought;
To set my mind fast upon thee,
And not to hang upon the blast of men's mouths;
To be content to be solitary;
Not to long for worldly company;
Little and little utterly to cast off the world,
And rid my mind of all the business thereof;
Not to long to hear of any worldly things,
But that the hearing of worldly phantasies may be
    to me displeasant;
Gladly to be thinking of God,
Piteously to call for his help;
To lean unto the comfort of God,
Busily to labour to love him;
To know mine own vileness and wretchedness,
To humble and meeken myself under the mighty
    hand of God;
To bewail my sins passed;

For the purging of them patiently to suffer
   adversity;
Gladly to bear my purgatory here;
To be joyful of tribulations;
To walk the narrow way that leadeth to life,
To bear the cross with Christ;
To have the last thing in remembrance,
To have ever afore mine eye my death that is ever
   at hand;
To make death no stranger to me,
To foresee and consider the everlasting fire of hell;
To pray for pardon before the judge come,
To have continually in mind the passion that
   Christ suffered for me;
For his benefits uncessantly to give him thanks,
To buy the time again that I before have lost;
To abstain from vain confabulations,
To eschew light foolish mirth and gladness;
Recreations not necessary, to cut off;
Of worldly substance, friends, liberty, life and all,
   to set the loss at right nought for the winning
   of Christ;
To think my most enemies my best friends,
For the brethren of Joseph could never have done
   him so much good with their love and favour as
   they did him with their malice and hatred.
These minds are more to be desired of every man
   than all the treasure of all the princes and kings,
   christian and heathen, were it gathered and laid
   together all upon one heap.

*This Prayer and Examination of Conscience
was written by Sir Thomas
after he had been condemned to die*

OUR FATHER    HAIL MARY    I BELIEVE

O Holy Trinity, the Father, the Son and the Holy
Ghost, three equal and co-eternal Persons and one
Almighty God, have mercy on me, vile, abject,
abominable, sinful wretch, meekly acknowledging
before thine high majesty my long continued sin-
ful life, even from my very childhood hitherto:
In my childhood . . . (in this and that point)
After my childhood . . .
And so forth by every age . . .

Now, good gracious Lord, as thou givest me the
grace to acknowledge them, so give me thy grace,
not only in word but in heart also, with very
sorrowful contrition, to repent them and utterly
forsake them.

And forgive me those sins also, in which by
mine own default through evil affections and evil
custom, my reason is with sensuality so blinded
that I cannot discern them for sin. And illumine,
good Lord, mine heart, and give me thy grace to

know them and to acknowledge them, and forgive me my sins negligently forgotten, and bring them to my mind with grace to be purely confessed of them.

Glorious God, give me from henceforth the grace, with little respect unto the world, to set and fix firmly my heart upon thee, that I may say with thy blessed apostle Paul: 'The world is crucified to me and I to the world' (Gal. 6, 14). 'To me to live is Christ and to die is gain. I desire to depart and to be with Christ' (Phil. 1, 21, 23).

Give me the grace to amend my life and to have an eye to mine end without grudge of death, which to them that die in thee, good Lord, is the gate of a wealthy life.

## Acts of Sorrow
## Faith Hope and Charity

Almighty God, teach me to do thy will (Ps. 142). O glorious God, all sinful fear, all sinful sorrow and pensiveness, all sinful hope, all sinful mirth and gladness take from me. And on the other side, concerning such fear, such sorrow, such heaviness, such comfort, consolation and gladness as shall be profitable for my soul, deal with me, Lord, according to thy great goodness.

Good Lord, give me the grace, in all my fear and agony, to have recourse to that great and wonderful agony that thou, my sweet Saviour, hadst at the Mount of Olivet before thy most bitter passion, and in the meditation thereof to conceive spiritual comfort and consolation for my soul.

Almighty God, take from me all vainglorious minds, all appetites of mine own praise, all envy, covetousness, gluttony, sloth and lechery, all wrathful affections, all appetite of revenging, all desire or delight of other folk's harm, all pleasure in provoking any person to wrath and anger, all delight of exprobration[1] or insultation[2] against any person in their affliction and calamity.

And give me, good Lord, a humble, lowly, quiet, peacable, patient, charitable, kind, tender and pitiful mind, with all my works, and all my words, and all my thoughts, to have a taste of the Holy Blessed Spirit.

Give me, good Lord, a full faith, a firm hope, and a fervent charity; a love to thee, good Lord, incomparable above the love to myself, and that I love nothing to thy displeasure, but everything in an order to thee.

Give me, good Lord, a longing to be with thee, not for the avoiding of the calamities of this wretched world, nor so much for the avoiding of the pains of purgatory, nor of the pains of hell neither, nor so much for the attaining of the joys of heaven in respect of mine own commodity, as even for a very love to thee.

[1] Reproachful accusation.     [2] Abusive treatment.

And bear me, good Lord, thy love and favour, which thing my love to theeward, were it never so great, could not but of thy great goodness deserve.

And pardon me, good Lord, that I am so bold to ask such high petitions, being so vile a sinful wretch and so unworthy to attain the lowest. But yet, good Lord, such they be as I am bound to wish, and should be nearer the effectual desire of them if my manifold sins were not the hindrance. From which, O glorious Trinity, vouchsafe of thy goodness to wash me with that blessed blood that issued out of thy tender body, O sweet Saviour Christ, in the divers torments of thy most bitter passion.

Take from me, good Lord, this lukewarm fashion, or rather key-cold manner of meditation and this dulness in praying unto thee. And give me warmth, delight and quickness in thinking upon thee.

And give me thy grace to long for thine holy sacraments, and specially to rejoice in the presence of thy very blessed body, sweet Saviour Christ, in the holy sacrament of the altar, and duly to thank thee for thy gracious visitation therewith, and at that high memorial with tender compassion to remember and consider thy most bitter passion.

Make us all, good Lord, virtually participant of the holy sacrament this day, and every day make us all lively members, sweet Saviour Christ, of thine holy mystical body, thy Catholic Church.

We pray you, Lord, to guard us from falling into
  sin today.

Have mercy on us, Lord, have mercy.

May your mercy rest upon us for we have trusted
  in you.

In you, Lord, have I put my trust, never let it be
  in vain.

Pray for us, holy Mother of God

That we may be made worthy of the promises of
  Christ.

## FOR FRIENDS

Almighty God, have mercy on N. . . and N. . .
(with special meditation and consideration of every
friend as godly affection and occasion requireth).

## FOR ENEMIES

Almighty God, have mercy on N. . . and N. . .
and on all that bear me evil will and would do me
harm, and their faults and mine together, by such
easy, tender, merciful means as thine infinite wisdom can best devise, vouchsafe to amend and
redress, and make us saved souls in heaven together, where we may live and love together with

thee and thy blessed saints, O glorious Trinity
for the bitter passion of our sweet
Saviour Christ.
AMEN

## FOR GRACE

Lord, give me patience in tribulation
and grace in everything to conform
my will to thine, that I may truly say:
*Fiat voluntas tua sicut in coelo et in terra.*

The things, Good Lord, that I pray for
give me thy grace to labour for.